D1366724

Creative
MANAGEMENT*

Creative
MANAGEMENT*

Wm. A. Marsteller

*A Euphemism for Common Sense

CRAIN
BOOKS

Published by Crain Books
A Division of Crain Communications, Inc.
740 Rush Street
Chicago, IL 60611

82   83   10 9 8 7 6 5 4 3 2

ISBN   0-87251-061-1
Library of Congress Catalog Card Number   81-66510

Printed in the United States of America

Contents

Contents

Managing Creativity and Similar Wishful Thinking 33

Setting Standards, Following Standards 45

Hiring, Firing and Retiring 63

Contents

Advice to the Young and Such of the Old Who May Never Learn 117

Left-Over Thoughts on Professional Communications 131

Preface

Bill Marsteller "retired" December 21, 1979, from Marsteller, Inc., the advertising and public relations agency he launched in 1951. The key word in that sentence wears quotation marks because none of us who have known and worked with Bill through the years can think of his departure from the business as anything other than a transfer of his intelligence and energy from running a communications agency to other activities associated with his lively and diverse interests.

This selection from Bill's writings is sponsored by his closest associates, members of the Marsteller Board of Directors. We have a simple reason for doing this. We think he said and wrote some things that deserve to be preserved and made available for others to read because they are not only interesting in themselves, but also valuable in transmitting wisdom and provoking fresh thinking.

This book is not a memorial or a commemoration or a testament. Bill despised all such rites and ceremonials and would not lend himself to them. We regard it rather as a celebration—a celebration of the ideas and words of one whom we have known as a superb manager and communicator and an equally superb developer of mangement and communication skills in his associates.

In his leadership of a successful business, he exemplified

the truth of the proposition that effective communication is a critical element in successful management. He knew how to instruct, persuade and motivate. He knew how important communication is in dealing with organizational subordinates, peers and superiors.

Since these are valuable resources for any manager, I believe that Bill's ideas about communication and the way he expresses his ideas can be studied with profit by managers in any organization.

Bill Marsteller possessed in himself and inspired in his associates, a dedication to unceasing striving for excellence. He did not believe that goal of excellence ever was or ever could be fully attained because he treated each progressive level of accomplishment as a new foundation for further progress toward an even higher goal. He nurtured, motivated, demanded with such persuasiveness and power that his dedication has been built enduringly into the organization he established and led. His name is not only on the door. It is embedded in the minds and attitudes and commitment of the people who continue to be Marsteller, Inc., after his departure.

Bill's concept of excellence in communications is grounded in a few basic ideas. These ideas are woven through the pieces collected in this book.

Here are a few of the things Bill taught me in many informal conversations about the art of getting an idea from one brain to another accurately and persuasively:

1. *The writer or speaker must know precisely what he or she wants to communicate.* The message must be stripped of irrelevancies, intellectual fogginess and all kinds of excess baggage. If the central idea isn't absolutely clear to the writer or speaker, it will never come through clearly to the reader or listener.

2. *A communicator must know the audience:* who they are, what they know or believe about the subject. Knowing the target audience also means knowing the vocabulary, the illustrations and examples, the relevant experiences that will be meaningful, empathetic, arousing to the audience.

3. *The structure of the communication* must include all the following key elements: capture of attention—engagement of self-interest—clear and powerful exposition of central idea—rational sequence of thought—reinforcing and action-oriented close.

4. Transformation of pedestrian, dull expression into vivid, informative, engaging, persuasive communication is accomplished through *the discipline of review, criticism, revision,* and in no other way.

Bill Marsteller knew, practiced and taught these fundamentals. He loved words with the love of a craftsman for his tools.

I think this book cannot fail to provide interesting and valuable ideas and examples for all managers who know that effective communication is essential in carrying out management's primary task—getting work done through other people who clearly understand what is wanted and are powerfully motivated to do it.

Melvin Anshen
Paul Garrett Professor
of Public Policy and
Business Responsibility
Graduate School of Business
Columbia University
and
Director, Marsteller Inc.

Introduction and Author's Cop-Out

For the person who loves to innovate, the person who is not afraid to doubt the past and test the future, the person who would rather have his or her name on a patent than a policy, it looks like a pretty good time to be around.

Since I have quite a few miles on me, some of my associates decided that a classy way to suggest a new and less authoritarian life style for myself was to bring out another book of the memos and other self-assured pronouncements I have issued from time to time, dealing with business, management, and personal development.

I say "another" book because they tried the same thing several years ago. That collection was called "The Wonderful World of Words." Unfortunately for my said associates, the conspiracy failed that time because I began to believe the title and kept on committing memoranda and such at a stepped-up pace.

Truth is, I have been writing this sort of thing to my corporate loved ones ever since I got the combination to the company safe. My theory is that if there is to be a reasonable unity of purpose and understanding among employees, then it is the responsibility of the chief executive officer to enunciate continuously the company's plans, programs, principles, and objectives.

The pieces selected by the editors for reproduction herein tend to be those that, however vaguely, talk about business management in its various manifestations. That naturally raises questions about the author's qualifications.

Let us be frank: They are minimal. They are also mostly borrowed, stolen, or simply discovered in the course of mingling. All I have been doing is setting forth the opinionated conclusions of one person and one company, to be accepted or ignored, unless you work with me, in which case the choice is more limited.

Once upon a time the General Electric Company had an electrical engineer named Morehead Wright whom they put in charge of manpower development, which, had Eleanor Holmes Norton been around then, would have been called personpower development to avoid a lawsuit by the Equal Employment Opportunity Commission. Anyway, old Morehead had heavy experience and a second helping of common sense, the latter being a commodity not regularly on sale in the employee development dodge. I think his

wisdom was about 99.44 percent pure and still floats today.
Among the things he said were:

- Personal development is an individual matter because everyone is unique.
- The motivation, desire, effort, obligation, and responsibility for vocational growth lie within the individual.
- Whom you work for is the most important factor in management development.
- There is no set of "ideal" personality traits for achievers.
- Because none of us is smart enough to predict long-range individual accomplishment with high accuracy, the opportunity for development in a company must be universal.

To these, I would add another:

- It helps to beat hell to be fortunate enough to be in the right place under the right circumstances at the right time.

It is because I have been fortunate in these respects, over and over through the years, that I have been able to observe the truth of Morehead Wright's canons.

First of all, I was fortunate enough to be in high school and college during the Great Depression and to have had to work full time. I was absorbing theory and practice simultaneously and learned that ultimately all development is self-development.

My job while in school was on the editorial staff of a very professional and highly profitable daily newspaper, *The Champaign-Urbana (Ill.) News-Gazette*. My boss for six years was a great editor, leader and role model, Edwin N. Jacquin. He ignored my still-oozing acne and gave me a lot of responsibility and treated me like I was mature, which certainly speeded the process. Whom you work for is vital.

I was fortunate in that the *Chicago Daily News* did not

at the time pay reporters a thrilling salary. So I took a career turn and started selling life insurance for the Massachusetts Mutual. There I also was trained to give aptitude tests to new agents and learned that winners and losers often sound alike, look alike and smell alike, but have an elusive difference of purpose and perseverance that resists typecasting.

World War the Second came along, and I was fortunate again: the armed services decided I had some impediments to usefulness in their scheme of things, so I got a job in a defense industry. As the more virile employees, one by one, got enthusiastic invitations from their draft boards to travel, by default I wound up in charge of advertising, bulletin boards, employee motivation, labor negotiations, ethnic weddings, some sales, and entertaining government expediters. During this time, I learned that everyone is damned well unique and that chocolate chip cookies don't do a lot as a development incentive for a Lithuanian welder.

When the war wound down, the company was merged into what became Rockwell International. My good fortune held out because they were sans ad manager and tapped me for the job. One day I was sitting in a meeting trying not to be noticed so I wouldn't be asked any of the 1,000 or so relevant questions I would be unable to answer when Colonel Willard F. Rockwell got into a dialogue with a regional sales manager, who was trying to persuade the colonel that the company should tool up to build a certain type of water meter.

"How many can you sell?" the Colonel asked.

"A hell of a lot," said the regional manager.

"How many?" the Colonel persisted.

"Well," said the R.M., "I wouldn't want to put a number on it, but I'm sure we can sell a hell of a lot."

Colonel Rockwell exploded. "Goddamn it, Carl, a handful of wet cow turd isn't very much if you want to fertilize a 40-acre field, but if someone shoves it in your face, that's a hell of a lot."

That's how market research came to Rockwell. Because I was probably the least fully employed person at the meeting, I was appointed to set up a market research department to do whatever it was that market research did.

During the course of finding out, I made several long trips through the oil fields of Oklahoma, Texas, New Mexico and Louisiana with an itinerant Tulsa photographer named R. B. Ward who took pictures of the installations of our products. Driving along straight, seemingly endless roads, devoid of scenery, R. B. would occasionally break a long silence.

"Only six things I know much about," he would say. "Barbeque, chili, union suits, cosmetics salesladies, box cameras and Fraser automobiles. Which one you want to talk about?"

Like R. B. Ward, I am most comfortable discoursing about those matters with which I am most familiar—the operation of an advertising and public relations agency. It's not that it is so different from the operation of other businesses, and especially not so different from other types of labor-intensive service businesses. Nevertheless be warned that in these pages you will find that most of the observations about people, places, and things are rooted in the business of commercial persuasion.

I had no master plan to found an advertising agency. The Big Idea was to start a market research consultancy specializing in technical and scientific products and services. There were none such in 1950. Dick Christian, who was also at Rockwell, would join me. Before we left, Al Rockwell, with some sense of relief, threw a farewell party for us. That evening, somewhere near or under the bar, it was agreed that a peachy idea would be to consolidate the Rockwell advertising account in our new agency, if indeed we had one and it was any good. The next week, speaking rapidly and with great charm, we assembled some borrowed money and acquired two other principals who had very small but very good agencies that were in successful operation. Once again, the good fortune of the right time and place.

A year later, Rockwell bought a helicopter to shuttle executives among some remote plants, and Al Rockwell

6

asked us to publicize it. What he envisioned was a front cover on *Life* and *Time* and two pages in *Reader's Digest*. What we envisioned was disaster followed by catastrophe preceding dismissal and acute undernourishment. We needed a New York public relations type on whom we could lay off the assignment, preferably someone desperate enough to work cheap, quick and quiet. We wrote five suspects. Harold Burson answered first and got the job. Just fortune, I guess. Anyway it worked out and today only one, much older, public relations firm in all the world is bigger than we are. Give us just a little more time.

An advertising and public relations agency is a splendid catwalk from which to observe all kinds of businesses and all kinds of people. If you look and listen you come to know a lot about many companies and many industries. My good fortune has also held out so far as clients are concerned. A lot of what I think I know is their fault. A few, in particular, must share some of the responsibility for my business beliefs as well as my concept of what makes a leader.

In a few cases, I observed how a real turkey sometimes, somehow, achieves a position from which genuine chaos can be created, often with tragic human consequences. In nearly all such situations Thanksgiving finally comes, but not always soon enough.

Our first large clients were Rockwell Manufacturing and the Clark Equipment Company, and Colonel Rockwell and George Spatta, the respective chairmen, were powerful influences. Both were physically rugged, impatient and driving and they scared the bejeezus out of most people. To us, however, they were interested and supportive and very much involved in our work for their companies. Both were builders and we grew with them—in experience, confidence, and in financial strength.

The two best modern management leaders I've worked with were with two wildly different companies.

Bob Hulsen was with the Moorman Manufacturing Company in Quincy, Ill., a privately owned corporation that sells animal feed and feed additives, farm to farm. Bob,

I think, knows more than anyone I've encountered about how to get all kinds of people working together at high levels of inherent ability with a sense of purpose and pleasure. Bob's secret is no secret. The American Management Associations can sell you 100 books that catalog every technique that Brother Hulsen uses. With him, though, it all comes alive because of his obvious, deeply felt enthusiasm, sincerity and belief. What I've learned from Bob Hulsen is: It don't mean a thing if you ain't got that swing.

IBM is the apparent antithesis of Moorman—highly visible, international, huge, spilling over with sophisticated people who have been trained in everything from art appreciation to zymurgy. Yet the two companies are very alike in their ability to develop a certain kind of person to an extraordinary level of management excellence. At the very top, IBM is the Fort Knox of business management talent, but the best and brightest during my years of association with the company was Gilbert E. Jones.

Gil Jones's special skill was as a friendly but unrelenting questioner. From him I learned the essentiality of fact gathering and preparation. I also learned that it is quite possible to be courteous, warm and very demanding simultaneously and that nearly everyone accepts a leader who is fully aware that that's what he is and is quite comfortable in that role.

My good fortune has certainly included my closest associates, especially Dick Christian and Harold Burson. Surely the three of us, who have recently shared the Office of the Chief Executive, give credence to Morehead Wright's point that it takes all kinds.

Unlike most closely held agencies, we've had outside directors for many years and never replaced any of them. Mel Anshen, Bill McNeill, Joe Wilkerson, Jim Hayes and Bill Cole have kept me from making an ass of myself many times and, on other occasions, sometimes led the cheers. Everyone needs a scorekeeper; most of us can use a confessor; even the Dallas Cowboys profit from cheerleaders.

All of our company's main sources of goods and services have been with us from the start and have been teachers as much as suppliers, especially Wally Vartan, LeRoy Martin, John Wrenn, Jim Challifoux, Harvey Peate, and Bill McNeill. We don't accept presents from them, but we take their counsel freely.

Finally, to get back to the contents of this book, you should be warned that a few of the items were included in the earlier tome and are being repeated. However, so that you will not be put in double jeopardy, any such outbursts are identified as repeats, just as in *TV Guide*.

You're on your own.

Bill Marsteller

The Inexact Art
of Motivation and
Personal Development

It's important to see the difference between leadership
and management. Some institutions are well managed
but poorly led. That is a mating that begets mediocrity.

The only useful definition of a leader is the simplest
one: A leader is someone who has followers.

Creative Management

No "average" man or woman can be a successful manager. Average is a number. A number has

No hands to reach out to help.
No heart to beat faster at the success of someone you
have helped.
No soul to suffer a bit when one of your people suffers.

An average lacks the disciplined mind to be tough and the self-confident strength to be gentle.

* * * *

It is easy to say of a person, or a company, or an industry that success came because of great talent, or fortuitous timing, or similar uncontrollable factors. This is a comfortable rationalization because it fits us all and forgives us equally. Unfortunately for our peace of mind, it just isn't true.

Rationalizing is like taking drugs. Responsibility for your own acts mists away. Rationalizing is always done sitting or lying down, never while walking hurriedly. Through some biological quirk, it is almost impossible to walk fast and at the same time feel sorry for yourself, or admit impotency, or accept a position of inferiority. The trick, then, is somehow to walk fast all the time. Satchel Paige said, "Never look back; something may be gaining on you."

* * * *

Some physiologist has informed us that muscle grows at one-tenth the speed of fat and one-one-thousandth the rate of cancer's spread. That probably explains all the publicity about Arnold Schwarzenegger.

* * * *

I am a firm believer in long-range planning. Every business will be better managed if it engages in this kind of future shock, understanding of course that all long-range plans must be regularly updated in line with reality.

12

Years ago I went to an American Management Association seminar on long-range planning, at which one company president debunked the whole idea because, he said, life is too uncertain.

The leader claimed that uncertainty was exactly what made long-range planning desirable and that as conditions changed, you adjusted your strategy.

He illustrated his point by telling about the visionary woman who, in sequence, married a banker, actor, preacher, and mortician as she entered different stages of life.

One for the money, two for the show, three to make ready and four to go.

* * * *

All of us by nature easily fall in love with our own ideas, our own words. Excellence is born of intelligent criticism. And maturity is the product of the self-confidence that seeks, accepts, and benefits from criticism. To avoid it is a symptom of personal weakness or low ability or both.

* * * *

Maybe you've heard this rhyme:

Everyone said it couldn't be done
And the odds were so great, who wouldn't?
But I tackled the job that couldn't be done,
And what do you know—it couldn't.

That is why there comes a time when most people should terminate their kid's violin lessons and quit trying to tell funny stories when they make a speech.

* * * *

Incompetence is as visible as excellence; laziness is as evident as dedication. A non-performer is generally as popular as a pigeon with diarrhea at a Keep America Beautiful picnic.

Managing and Motivating People

Will Rogers used to start all his monologues, "All I know is what I read in the papers."

All I know about managing and motivating people is either from reading books or out of my experience with successes and failures.

There is no easy way to become an excellent manager.

First of all, it is not inherited, and that's the easiest way to become anything. Some tendencies toward being a good manager may be inherited, although I have never found out what they are. Mostly, being a good manager is simply discipline. That means that there is hope for all of us, however far we have already strayed.

Let us start down this list of how to become a great manager.

1. *You must lead, not push.* That means involvement. Most of all, you have to be a part of the whole thing. It's the opposite of the let's-you-and-him-do-it syndrome. You know: "Let's-you-and-him-go-out-and-see-the-plant-and-see-if-you-can-straighten-that-out."

The first secret of good management is to get people to believe you are a good manager, whether indeed you are or not. When you want somebody to do something, you should go with them. I think it's let's-you-and-me instead of let's-you-and-him.

2. *Delegate.* The world is full of people who will screw up a one-car funeral. If you delegate to such a person any very substantial job, the chances are good you will be in serious trouble. Unless you take the time to explain the route—that the cemetery is in Queens, but that Queens is reached over any one of four bridges, and that the bridge you'd like this funeral to take is a certain bridge—there's always a possibility that the corpse will go one way and the family will go another. So I suggest that when you get carried away by books that tell you the job of a manager is to delegate, *you must delegate with an explanation.*

I get a little bit concerned when we get so caught up in what the textbooks say that we don't watch the details ourselves. If we delegate and don't follow through, then we are in Deepest Trouble, which is even farther out than Deepest New Jersey.

3. The only way to know what's going on is to *get out of your own office*. I think you have to meet the troops in the field. We have had managers at many levels who are perfectly prepared to participate in any war that breaks out as long as it breaks out in their own office. The trouble is, of course, that a lot of the problems don't happen in your office. They occur someplace else, and unless you circulate a bit, the chances are very good that people will not bring those problems to you. The finest prospects for Preparation H are the people who spend most of their time in their own offices.

I will tell you something that most of you do not believe. *Everyone who works for you is, to one degree or another, afraid of you.* It's been a hard lesson for me to learn that anybody could be afraid of me.

The truth is that every one of you has some people who are afraid of you. They will not come to you with their problems. You think that they love you and they trust you. Neither one is true. You are not nearly as wonderful to the people who work for you as you think you are.

4. *Ask for trouble; ask for help.* The greatest need of a manager is two-way communication. If you can set up the kind of atmosphere where people do come to you for help, if you can break down the barriers so that people actually are reasonably comfortable with you, you are far ahead.

Remember this: All people like to be consulted. You like to be consulted by your boss. All of your people like to be consulted by you.

5. *Consistency, thou art a gem.* Emerson wrote, "Consistency is the hobgoblin of little minds," but it really isn't at all.

Consistency is what all of your people want badly, and I say this with conviction because I have lived with lots of inconsistent managers.

We once changed a general manager because three of his people who worked directly for him said, "He goes or we go!" We asked, "What's the problem?" We listened for half an hour, and the problem was that on Monday, Wednesday, and Friday, they got a hot poker. On Tuesday and Thursday they got love and affection. They were not willing to become Pavlov's dog.

The hot shower/oak-leaf flogging/cold shower routine may be great for the Finns, but they are a dolorous people. Whether your natural style is ebullience or aloofness is far less important than if whatever you are, you are most of the time. We all need security in our employer-employee relationships. Morale is shattered by uncertainty. So, if you're a son-of-a-bitch, be a son-of-a-bitch all the time.

When you become a manager, you give up the right to be moody. The antidote for moodiness is self-quarantine. All of us are a little moody at times, so stay by yourself until you get over it.

Moodiness is an emotion that affects others. Fortunately nearly all emotions can be controlled. Psychiatrists would starve to death if they hadn't sold the world that emotions can be controlled. Moodiness is low on the scale and can be kept hidden.

6. *Remember the Gettysburg Address.* Lincoln not only said "all men are created equal," but he also said "I would not be a slave, so I would not be a master." One of the biggest problems in management is favoritism. It can be real or it can be imagined, and it doesn't make a lot of difference which it is.

You are on dangerous ground if you pick your closest friends from a few of those whom you manage.

Apart from creating a clique or claque, you are likely to start making biased decisions. Those you like are not always right and those you don't like are not always wrong. The validity of an idea has little to do with the charm of its sponsor.

The appearance of favoritism by a manager also can lead to legal problems these days. Equal opportunity is both a sound management principle and the law. I have been helped by remembering what Mark Twain said years ago: "I do not care about a man's color, religion, or nationality; as long as he's a member of the human race, that's bad enough for me."

7. *Listen here!* Listening is a skill. I am very conscious of this because it is the biggest problem I've had in my entire business career.

Some of my close associates know that for many years I've written notes to myself that say such things as "Shut up!" I put them in my pockets and pull them out from time to time. I used to write little signs and put them in front of me: "Let someone else talk."

You need to listen to clients. If you listen to clients instead of talk to clients, it takes a long while for them to find you out. Listening and observing are the basics behind the learning process.

8. *Don't throw away your most becoming suit.* If you've been the account executive and now you are management but the client still expects you instead of somebody else, what do you do? I'm afraid the answer is that you keep on being the account executive on those accounts as long as you live and as long as you stay in the business.

It's like this: Once upon a time a man was driving along a country road and he came to a little girl, perhaps five, leading an immense, mean-looking bull. He stopped and asked her what she was doing.

She said, "I'm leading the bull down to the pasture to the cow."

And the man said, "But can't your father do that?"

And she said, "Nope. Only the bull."

One of the things that goes with any personal service business, whether you're a lawyer, or a management consultant, or whatever, is that you still have to show up on those early, original accounts for the rest of your life. The more regularly you do it, the better off you are. And not only that, but the more respect they'll have for the people you supervise. You know, the greatest thing in the world for a creative person—for Bill Bernbach, for David Ogilvy, for anyone like that—is to still write an ad and be able to tell everyone, "I did it myself." Whatever you're doing well, find time to keep on doing it.

Leo Burnett said in a famous speech, "Finally, somebody has to get out the ads." It is easy to hire an office full of people who are very good at meeting-going. It is difficult to hire people who can leave a meeting and get something done immediately thereafter. If you can quickly translate what happened at that meeting into a finished product, you are a precious person and will always be so perceived.

9. *Always tell the truth.* When you start giving stories to the people who work for you that turn out to be fantasies, you might as well move someplace else because you've fouled your nest and the odor will cling to your clothes.

10. *Stand for something.* There were these two old guys who met every day in front of the Plaza Hotel in New York. They would sit side by side and say very little for hours at a time. Finally, one of them said to the other one, "Life is like a fountain." After a long pause, the other said, "So, why is life like a fountain?" After an even longer pause, the first one said, "Well, maybe you're right; maybe life is not like a fountain."

That's the problem with so many men and women today. Stand for something. Take a clearly understood position, even if it's only the concept of being revolted by ankle socks.

Think out what you're for and stay with it. Find your principles, big or small. Set your own high standards and establish with the people you supervise that you have a very low tolerance for the mundane.

11. *Avoid cheap praise.* Praise makes good men better and bad men worse.

A year ago I wrote to all our general managers and said I would give a bottle of the best booze money could buy to anyone who could write 12 monthly reports without saying anything about "rave reviews." I am sick to the death of cheap praise. Some of those rave reviews, when you read them carefully, are really only saying that someone licked the envelopes nicely without getting spit on the address. I often read rave reviews of someone doing something that is about 30 percent below the level of work for which he was hired. You save praise for the truly extraordinary.

Jonathan Swift said,

" 'Tis an old maxim in the schools,
That flattery's the food of fools;
Yet now and then your men of wit
Will condescend to take a bit."

12. *Be there when no one else wants to be there.* A few years ago, the United States celebrated its 200th anniversary, and one of our clients was sold by one of our bright management people on a great program that had nothing to do with the bicentennial except that it was to be available the first week in July. So he arranged for two service departments to work the entire Fourth of July weekend while everyone else in the company was off celebrating. Fifteen people sweated out Saturday and Sunday in the office, but the manager wasn't there. His days of management were, for all practical purposes, over. He'd lost the support of the troops. If you want people to work at an odd time, the way to get ahead is to be there with them, just as odd as the rest.

I'm astonished by what's going on around the world today on Friday afternoons. I think that the manager who really wants to make a point with his people, if not indeed with his management, is the manager who doesn't bust his ass or her derrière to duck out early. Managers who are still there on Friday afternoons or who work the occasional weekend make a great point.

Going in now and then on the weekend has many rewards. There is so much to see. Walking around, looking around, seeing who's there and who isn't, who was there and who wasn't. It is a time to contemplate—to contemplate your work area, to contemplate your job, to contemplate your people.

Over the years, many times when I've gone into the office on a Saturday, I could see creative people who were working their tails off for someone else on the weekend. If only some of those people for whom they were working so hard would turn up on a Saturday and say to them, "Thank you for helping me out." What an influence this would have!

It's also an excuse to get out of the house if your mother-in-law comes visiting.

13. *Get a complete managerial once a year.* It is like a complete physical. At least once a year you need an evaluation a lot more than your people do because, like an audit or a physical examination, it is something that ought to happen to everybody occasionally.

I think managerial ego is similar to the dampness that fogs the mirror on a warm, humid day after you've taken a shower. We all need criticism, every one of us. We all need a diagnostician, and the higher up you get, the more you need one.

I am concerned more and more about the managers I meet who I feel are headed for a very early death. They are so self-impressed I think it is inevitable that sooner or later they're going to go for an afternoon walk and get hit by a motorboat.

If you know who you are, there's a chance to do something about it. There is an old Talmudic story that there was an Oriental king who heard that Moses was kindly and generous and a bold leader. And so he had Moses' portrait brought to his astrologers and phrenologists to examine. They looked at the portrait and said that, on the contrary, Moses was cruel and greedy and craven and self-seeking. And so the king went to Moses and saw that he was good and said, "My astrologers and phrenologists were wrong."

But Moses disagreed; he said they were right. "They saw what I was made of, but they couldn't tell you how I struggled against that so that I would become what I am."

Most managers are managers in part. In part, because of their own ability and their own makeup, their own aggressiveness, their own self-sacrifice, their own brains and so forth. But also, in part, because of luck.

I knew a guy once who became very successful and he said, "I was very lucky." And one of the people who worked for him said, "I think that's exactly correct. You were lucky. I never had it that good. With my luck, if I'd have been Sophia Loren's baby, I would have been bottle fed."

As a young newspaper reporter, I once interviewed Bob

Zuppke, the great Illinois football coach, on the eve of a championship game. It had been raining for 24 hours and the field was bound to be muddy. I asked Zup if that would be an advantage or a disadvantage to his team. And he said, "When it rains, it rains on both teams 50-50, and they both play with the same ball."

14. *Remember, all of us have much for which to be modest.*

He thought he'd quit the squad because
He didn't like the system.
"They'll howl and cry and plead," he said.
But, shucks, they never missed him.

When I hear of problems related to supposedly indispensable people, I have to think that maybe we have some absolutely invaluable people, but I don't know who they are. I think all of us have much for which to be modest. If we all believe that, then working together, leaning on each other, we'll do pretty well and have a good time doing it.

A Test for High-Potential Employees

There was a time when conventional management dogma held that any company that was well run must develop a list of its "high-potential" people and concentrate its tender loving care on those few anointed specimens.

We made up such lists for a few years until, as time went by, we began to wonder how we could be so wrong so often. We thought it was just us until two very highly regarded corporations publicly confessed at personnel meetings that they, too, were in a batting slump and that some line-up changes had been made at Armonk and Schenectady.

The trouble is that the most obvious signs for identifying young hotshots are often red herrings.

For instance, we run many training seminars and in every one of them, a few highly vocal types stand out and you begin to equate visibility with vision and noise with knowledge. Some people are natural-born reciters and get their exercise by waving their arms to be recognized. Alas, our clients pay us nothing for excellence in seminar going, so long ago we quit making personnel judgments on the basis of meeting participation. Every company has some able senior managers who are by nature rather quiet. Sometimes the meek do indeed inherit the earth.

Another frequently misleading measure is what someone did elsewhere. Skills are not always transferable. A concert pianist, however acclaimed, is not terribly useful in a marching band.

The most unreliable test of all is how someone looks. I remember one gorgeous young man we had who, you could tell just by looking at him, was going to be perfect sitting on the dais waiting to receive his award as the Anti-Defamation League Man of the Year in Advertising and Allied Arts. The trouble was that when it came to getting the world's work done, he was always eighteen and a half miles out of Peoria with a flat tire.

There are behavioral psychologists on the loose with red beards and copyrighted aptitude tests, and I guess every manager is tempted to try them once. I can only tell you that at General Electric, out of 143 carefully screened crown princes and princesses, only 37 percent achieved the success predicted for them. And I can tell you that the Massachusetts Mutual Life Insurance Company trained me to give those tests and that after two years and a couple hundred guinea pigs I told my general agent that I had no confidence in the results.

The only reliable guide I know to future potential is intelligence. That alone isn't enough, but its absence is very hard to offset.

You want to know who I think has high potential?

You. Whomever you are. Very few of us ever come close to developing our resources to the limit. Therefore, any personal development program ought to be nearly universal and individual evaluations should be made and remade from puberty to senility.

Some People Have All the Luck

Gary Player, the professional golfer, was having a particularly successful run of tournaments. He was making incredible putts, sinking shots from off the green, going hole after hole without so much as even stepping off the fairways.

Several writers and sports announcers marveled at his streak of luck.

Gary answered them: "It's funny—the harder you work, the luckier you get."

There is no question that luck plays a part in many of life's successes.

George Spatta, who came from the most humble of backgrounds to become the highly paid chairman of Clark Equipment Company, told me how he got his first promotion. "I was just lucky," he said. "I'd been working on a patent application for an axle housing I'd designed and I just couldn't get it finished during the day. One night about midnight I looked up and Eugene Clark, the boss, was standing there. He'd been working late getting ready for a board of directors' meeting the next day and saw my light. He looked over the drawings I was working on and asked me to come before the board the next day and tell them about the patent application."

The patent was granted and has been worth millions to Clark Equipment. George was very lucky.

Maybe truck axles have something to do with luck. I've heard Colonel W. F. Rockwell, who founded what is now Rockwell International, tell this story about his early days. He'd scraped together all the cash he had, borrowed all he could, and, barely 20 years old, bought control of the Wisconsin Axle Company, a small enterprise near bankruptcy. At the end of the first year, he and his company were financially exhausted, and he celebrated Christmas by being unable to meet the payroll for his small staff. Between Christmas and New Year's, with a few more borrowed dollars, he set out to try once more to sell one of the handful of prospects he'd called on dozens of times before.

"I got lucky," the colonel recalled. "At Cortland, N.Y., I

persuaded the Brockway Truck Company to give us a trial order with an advance partial payment." The Colonel was often lucky after that, so much so that the Timkens bought him out to run their automotive parts business.

Two women were coming out of a concert by the graduates of the Julliard School of Music. One of them was ecstatic about the performance of a soloist who, the program notes said, had been studying the piano since she was three years old.

"Baloney," the other woman said. "If I had long fingers like her, I'd play that good, too."

Harold Burson, who runs our public relations company, is a lucky type, too. In late 1951, Dick Christian and I needed professional public relations assistance with a project. We got the names of five small New York PR firms, including Harold Burson Public Relations. We wrote all of them, outlining the job. Within two weeks we had letters from four of the firms bidding for the assignment. However, as luck would have it, Harold got on a train to see us in Chicago the day after he got our letter and by the time we heard from the others, we'd made a deal with him. He's often lucky like that.

Some people have all the luck. As Gary Player says, you can usually tell them by how hard they work at it.

Fables for Our Times:
A Simple Lesson in Egg Laying

Once upon a time there was a farmer with a coop full of chickens, including one rooster who, like a chairman of the board, didn't do much but still managed to avoid the coq au vin.

The rest of the chickens were expected to lay eggs. They went about it in different ways.

The happiest ones hopped on the nest, concentrated, got their business done, and had the most time left for sunshine and corn pecking.

Another group cackled a lot to each other first but ultimately got their eggs laid. There was a lot of envy in this group, and many a comparison was made both as to size and color. This led to a certain amount of nervousness since not all days are alike. You know how it is.

The last group had real trouble getting on with it at all. They got their share of corn all right and in fact got nice and plump since they tended to daydream on the nest when they should have been working. They developed a lot of personal hang-ups, including constipation.

Since all the chickens were Rhode Island Reds, they looked pretty much alike, but in time the farmer figured out which was which.

The first group got to have lunch with the rooster and kept on producing happily until they were fully vested.

The second group, mostly because they could see an ax on a stump just outside the coop, produced just enough to avoid a confrontation.

But the third group, alas, while they had nice feathers, sat on empty nests. They were replaced with layers. But in a fricassee you could never tell they hadn't hacked it.

MORAL: *Don't count your chickens; count the eggs.*

Planning for the Future

For many years we have had a corporate long-range plan.

A committee of the board updates it annually, projecting growth five years into the future. Income goals are then translated into estimated needs in terms of people, facilities, equipment and so on.

Because companies change as they mature, just as people do, the long-range plan changes, too. The thrust of our business is different than it was only a few years ago. The business climate in which we operate is different. We have to factor in our success and failures, raising our sights where we have exceeded our goals and either abandoning or stretching out accomplishment dates on projects that lag.

For a long-range plan to be something more than random wishes, it must be built from the bottom up. Consequently, we start with projections from each of our profit centers. These projections are tempered by past results and local opportunities.

Although most really well-managed corporations now operate with fairly well-conceived long-range plans, a large number of companies still have done little to anticipate their future. Customarily they say, "Our business is too different to do much long-range planning."

That's a cop-out and a sad commentary on the management sophistication of great segments of industry.

Now, carrying this stuffy message straight to you individually, a long-range plan is just as possible, just as valuable, for you as for a company. Your future, to a very large extent, depends on progress toward personal goals. Progress can't be measured until goals are set.

Personal goals are no more static than corporate goals. You'll change your objectives as you go along, just as companies do. The important thing is to know what your objectives are at any given time and what you're doing to achieve them.

Drifting is no more desirable for an individual than a company. In either case, it is likely to lead to unpleasant surprises, the frustration of lack of purpose, and eventually the atrophy of character.

Personal Agenda Positioning*

Mel Anshen once wrote a very funny paper on the fine art of agenda positioning in which he suggested some rules for keeping a committee or board or whatever from accomplishing anything.

---

*From "The Wonderful World of Words"

The secret is to put unimportant items at the top of the list so that most of the time is spent on such things as what paper stock to use for the new letterhead or whether to put rubies in the ten-year service pins. That way there will be no time left to cover important matters, and they'll be tabled until they simply disappear.

But you don't have to form a committee to achieve nonaccomplishment; you can do it on your own. In fact, many people do.

If you will just start each day gradually, filling in yesterday's time sheet, checking out the paint job in the rest room, rearranging your paper clip collection, and systematically reviewing what most of the office did last night, you should be able to build up a head of inertia that will last long enough so that it will be too late to start anything until tomorrow.

Once I thought I was lazy and had to impose some form of self-discipline to get anything done. Now I know everyone is; it's only a matter of degree.

I observe that productive, well-organized people are happy people and that people who just dawdle the days away are sour and self-accusatory.

For myself, the only way I can have a satisfying day is to start out with a list of things I want to or must do. I number them in a priority sequence and then start cleaning them off. What's left over, or added as the day goes on, is the basis for the next day's agenda. Finally things get done, more or less, or dropped. But, hopefully, it's the unimportant things that get shoved aside.

Now, isn't that a wholesome message?

The Benefits of Personal Research

It is a faded page in our corporate history, but our company actually started out as Marsteller Research, Inc. Advertising and public relations came some months later.

So I put myself among those who think that you ought to gather information before you start disbursing it. But I sometimes wonder how many people understand the enormous value of getting personally involved in the research.

Before me is some research from a farm publication on what interests the dairy farmer. Valid, no doubt, but I firmly believe that if you expect to create clear communication with said dairy farmer you've got to get out and do some cow mingling yourself. No report can ever bring home to you the problems and interests of these farmers as accurately as some time spent with them skidding around a few open-air bovine bathrooms.

When we put together a new business presentation, we normally do some research by way of preparation. I'm convinced that we are at our best when the people presenting the research have participated in its collection. There is something about having been to a dealer's showroom yourself, or having talked to some customers yourself, that shines through with conviction and legitimacy.

It is the difference between reading the script and going to the play.

There's a further reward in doing some of the field research yourself: It's often a lot of fun. Some of my fondest memories are of calling on industrial distributors in New Orleans, questioning water superintendents in Atlantic City, counting fire hydrants in Midland and Odessa, Texas, and collecting opinions on an inflatable life preserver from female lifeguards in Miami Beach. It is all part of a rich, full life and helps you build up a supply of anecdotes that can be embellished and exaggerated for years.

Thank God It's Monday

I'm not sure whether TGIF is known in other environments, but restless natives here, of course, know it stands for "Thank God It's Friday."

There is nothing wrong with being ready for a weekend away from the office. But there is something sad about those people who hate Monday because it starts another week of work.

I find that the happiest, best adjusted people are supporters of both TGIF and TGIM.

If you hate Mondays and therefore hate work, you ought to quit. You can marry rich or get by on welfare and begging. In either case, Fridays and Mondays apparently run together and lose significance.

I have always looked forward to work, which is a good thing because I have always had to work. Because work is a fact of life, I've always felt that anyone who is habitually unhappy is just a little bit sick. Of course, those people who are unhappy only because of their particular job, company, or boss are not so much sick as gutless.

Most successful people, I observe, come to terms with the reality of their own lives. They waste little time envying others who seem to have it easier, realizing that wishing for that which cannot be is a sure route to unhappiness or, at worst, emotional bankruptcy.

I like Fridays, but I also look forward to Mondays. Most weeks, to the other five days, too.

Thus spoke Pollyanna.

Old-Fashioned Personnel Policies

All of a sudden it seems to be popular for companies to go outside for key executives, bypassing men and women who have been around for years.

The rationale seems to be that an outsider will pump in new ideas, will bring along no prejudices or loyalties to impede personnel housecleaning, and will generally inject a healthy skepticism.

No doubt. But whether that's either good or needed would seem to depend upon the company and the way it planned for the future right along.

We remain firmly committed to the perhaps old-fashioned principle of promotion from within. We have gone outside very rarely to fill a key job and seldom with success. If we have to do it, we look upon it as a failure of the management to anticipate needs and problems and to recruit, train and retain the right people.

Management ability is part formalized training, part individual temperament and sensitivity, and part slowly gained on-the-job experience. The formalized training can probably be transferred from company to company. The personal qualities of leadership that have so much to do with management achievement are also largely portable. But the judgment and wisdom that comes from the time-consuming immersion into the peculiarities of a specific company in a specific industry are also a priceless part of the equation of success.

So we go our way, recruiting the best young people we can find, and running one of the most expensive in-house seminar training programs in the industry, and forcing managers all along the line into frequent hard-nosed personnel evaluations. Along the way we lose our share of people. But it's all worth it if, in the end, as the business grows and the need for management expands, the pool of available high-quality people keeps pace.

It's a policy we'll give up with great reluctance, regardless of what others do.

Which they probably do only because they have to.

Hidden Assets

In our business, good people are interesting, open people. There are all too many advertising and public relations people with polyester minds—permanently pressed and wrinkle resistant. They mouth the litany of the trade, but they create nothing but copies.

When I was young and couldn't sleep, I counted girls. When I got older and couldn't sleep, I replayed golf courses I had visited. Later on, I mentally started our company over and speculated on whom I would first try to persuade to join us again. Note that I never counted sheep. In my loneliest and most frustrated moments, I have never favorably fantasized sheep.

Anyway, of the first 10 or 20 or so people, I looked for the common thread. It is not age, sex, geography, tenure, job description, physical magnificence, or genius.

But they are all bright, and bright is good.

They are also loyal.

They like what they are doing, so they are enthusiastic and hard-working and dependable.

They all have a sense of humor and a reasonable degree of humility.

They tend to be free of self-deceit and have made peace with their strengths and weaknesses.

There is, of course, a set of antonyms.

As fellow students of the Bible, you will remember from Revelations that the Four Horsemen of the Apocalypse—the four major plagues of mankind—are war, famine, pestilence and death.

In our business, the four unchanging plagues are dullness, egotism, cynicism and pomposity.

Wordsworth wrote of a dullard: "A primrose by the river brim, a yellow primrose was to him and it was nothing more." In our business world, when imagination is lacking, ability is lacking.

Egotism begets isolation. Cynicism smothers originality. Whatever the pompous produce is buried under boredom. Any of these can be cancerous to the practice of communication.

In any company that aims for leadership, the search for and the development of unusual people must be first among corporate objectives.

The important assets of a company are not dollars in the bank or used furniture. They are not even the good will of a superior customer list although, as a president of U.S. Steel once said, "I would rather own a market than a mill."

The hidden asset that determines the real value of a company—that sets it apart from competition—is its people. The only companies that grow are those that expect their people to grow and spend the time and money and understanding to help them do it.

Managing Creativity and Similar Wishful Thinking

Happy companies are managed by people with hearts and souls as well as minds. They are led by people who would rather create than consume. They exude an aura of pride instead of prejudice. They are companies with people who are not bored with each other because they are not bored with themselves.

Creative Management

Let me give you my definition of creativity. I define creativity as what I think is creative.

* * * *

Technology and modern communications combine to get products accepted more quickly, copied more quickly, and replaced more quickly.

The creative person doesn't have time for foreplay. Today is the day. The time is now.

* * * *

The principles of superior communications are not really very clear or uniformly accepted. We know relatively little about why some speakers, writers or teachers are so much better than others even with the same input and training. It seems to me that the good communicator is one who first communicates well with himself or herself. This easy-to-understand person is one who instinctively alters, discards and replaces alternative distillations of meanings.

Communication is not just words, paint on canvas, math symbols or the equations and models of scientists; it is the inter-relation of human beings trying to escape loneliness, trying to share experience, trying to implant ideas.

* * *

It takes extraordinary effort and self-discipline for the small, modestly financed agency to be bright and fresh and imaginative while at the same time staying fiscally seaworthy. The fat float easily, but the thin have to kick a little.

* * *

In a manufacturing plant, the scrap heap is only rusting metal cuttings or porous castings or decomposing chemicals. In our business, the scrap heap is people and therefore far more precious. Our moral responsibility is much greater.

The Climate of Creativity*

Some of our management types have spent restless hours lately wondering if we have established the right climate for creativity.

This is nice. I like to see management types worry because as long as they trouble themselves with this kind of self-doubt, the company has a promising future.

On the other hand, I have some opinions about what constitutes a creative climate and how you go about producing creative rainfall.

First, from page 1 of Meteorology I, we find that if you drill wells in the desert, or if you seed cloudless skies, you get no water.

It's the same with creativity. You don't fill unimaginative and undermotivated people with cleverness and a drive for achievement by hocus-pocus with the working conditions. Bright lights don't make bright people.

It takes more than a forked stick and a confident manner to get steady work as a rainmaker. But because thirsty people get desperate, all kinds of fakers get temporary employment. If they are eccentric and wear black capes and have long hair and smell faintly of Monday's buttermilk, their moment of success may be hastened, for who among us is to separate the uncalculated trappings of genius from the neurotic adornments of self-deceit?

The salaried branches of creativity are infested with the same kind of transient quacks—men and women who have convinced themselves they are creative because they want to be. And for a while they are able to convince others by repeating out loud, over and over, "I am creative, I am creative, I am creative," all the while picking their noses in public to prove their disdain for convention.

Give the person who is fundamentally noncreative any climate you wish and you will not beget usable creation; give the pseudo-creative person the climate of his own de-

---

*From "The Wonderful World of Words"

vising, and he will reward you with a slow trickle of mean-
derings in derivative irrelevance, along with a steady flow
of abuse.

These types, who come and go in the creative craft,
building a list of credits for someone else's work, are not
really a part of the problem. The challenge is to take the
people who are creative, with either an active or latent
sense of usable invention, and to give them the atmosphere
in which to flourish. To stimulate them. To encourage
them. To reward them. To comfort and keep them.

But how? What common conditions, what combinations of thunderheads and sunshine produce the climate of
creativity?

For Ernie Pyle it was a battlefield, for Somerset
Maugham it was the luxury of the Riviera, for Winston
Churchill it was the quiet and austerity of his booklined
study, for Jimmy Breslin it was the clamorous city room of
a metropolitan newspaper. John O'Hara, a very wealthy
man, worked as long and as routine a daily schedule as an
insurance clerk despite the fact that he never needed to earn
another dollar.

There are those who say that creativity is lost in advertising and public relations because of deadlines and because of the volume of work to be done. Yet hundreds of
great reporters and columnists are regularly creative
against deadlines from which extensions are not granted. I
have a friend who has taught composition in a college of
music for many years. Every term students ask him for
additional time to submit their major work of the semester.
He says that never once has a superior work been submitted
after the original deadline; all the good stuff comes in on
time. It is the student who has nothing to say musically who
needs the extra time to say it.

Abe Burrows' fame as a play doctor comes from his
ability to create under extraordinary pressure, but James
Thurber turned out a prodigious flow of material with no
apparent pressure at all.

A few years ago, the five most creative advertising men

then in practice were probably Bill Bernbach, Fax Cone, George Gribben, Leo Burnett and Rosser Reeves, all inhabitants of the Copywriters Hall of Fame. In the offices they occupied, the way they dressed, their ability to speak in public, their political convictions, they differed widely.

What these five peers really had in common was a compulsion to create and a willingness to work hard at it. They did not need a certain kind of office, certain time of the day, phase of the moon, soft music, sharp pencils, three martinis, or light covering of dandruff in order to be inventive. Their fame is rooted in their ability to be fresh and interesting and relevant and original over a long period of time for a wide variety of purposes.

Dr. Donald W. Taylor of Yale University, who was one of the three or four psychological researchers who have made scientific studies in the field of creativity, finds the same thing about the Nobel prize winners he investigated in depth. He found that the temperament, education, physical characteristics, philosophical viewpoints and living and working conditions of these greatest of inventive geniuses were of as many patterns as there were people. The climate of creativity that nurtured them all was a purely personal one.

It is my conclusion that we cannot artificially impose a climate that will be automatically hospitable to all creative people.

We can and should recognize work that is truly creative, single it out for praise and reward, and constantly seek to stretch harder for more that is unique. We can, in short, *want* creativity and, wanting it very badly, we shall get more of it.

But at the same time, we cannot extinguish creative drive from those of our people who are genuinely creative. Creative people are self-driven, neither pushed nor towed. Their need for expression comes from within; their need for achievement can only be self-satisfied; their need to do something better and different than anyone else has ever done is the creative climate that motivates them best.

Who Really Are the Creative Ones?

There is a worldwide myth that creative people are in short supply. If "creative" is defined as producing unique ideas, then the myth is totally without foundation.

Once upon a time, Alex Osborne, the "O" of BBDO, got wide attention for promoting brainstorming as a creative process that would generate original thinking and tap the suppressed ideas of all types of people normally not thought of as creators of fantastic ideas. Mr. Osborne ran the Buffalo office of BBDO, and during the long winters there the citizenry is driven to peculiar pastimes.

But he did indeed prove that all kinds of people, if encouraged, can come up with some very *outrè* ideas. The trouble was, according to the testimony of many BBDO alumni of those times, few of the ideas were directly related to the problem at hand, and, worse, when an idea that was both relevant and practical spilled out, its proponent almost never had the ability to carry it to a usable conclusion.

Being creative is both pleasurable and easy, pretty much like sex. The labor pains come later. Or to draw an analogy from a different recreational form, Tommy Henrich, the one-time Yankee outfielder, said, "Catching a ball is fun; it's what you do with it after you catch it that's a business."

Over the years hundreds of client plans, department reports, and summaries of alleged accomplishments have passed over my desk. They tend to be grouped under three headings—"Proposed," "In Process," and "Completed." I have schooled myself to start reading from the bottom and stop altogether before I get to "Proposed." Anybody can propose. Witness the number of illogical marital couplings that go on every day.

The noble men and women of this world are those rare and wonderful ones who not only propose unique ideas but also have disciplined themselves to the patience, the sense of the imperative, the doggedness, and the often lonely drudgery of fulfillment. In the long run, they're the only ones who matter.

Communications' Barrier Reef

The hardest part of being in the communications business is facing up to the fact that most people have very little interest in being communicated with.

And the highest barriers are often erected by those who have been most successful, most widely accepted as authorities on something or other, most firmly established as leaders.

Probably it's because nothing is so threatening or disorienting as a new idea. Frequently a new idea means giving up an old one—one held long enough to be comfortable and habitual. So it follows that the established leader shuts off the intake of much communication by filling available time with an outgo of communications.

One day, no doubt, there will be widespread education in listening. Until that happy time, when more people are skilled audiences, the perceptive communicator must realize that anything designed as a monologue will have a low level of transmittal.

But isn't all advertising, aren't all feature stories or speeches monologues? Not so.

An advertisement that says, "For Over 50 Years, We've Been Giving Speech Lessons" is a monologue. An ad that asks, "Do You Make These Ten Common Mistakes in Speaking?" is a dialogue. The first approach, along with being dull, will ultimately present the idea in the midst of a lecture. The second will help the reader discover the new idea for himself from the storeroom of his own experience.

I read a lot of speeches. Nearly all of them are tedious, and their reason for being—the promulgation of a new idea or concept—is usually lost in the failure to make the point in a way that can be warmly comfortable or reassuring.

One of the most challenging creative technical men of recent years was Charles F. Kettering of General Motors. He was also one of the best communicators, because he understood that old thought patterns set up an instant obstacle to the ingestion of new concepts.

He loved to tell a story about a presentation he once

made on the practicality of the lightweight diesel engine. At the close, a man stood up and said, "You can't make the pistons of aluminum—the stresses are too great. It won't work."

Kettering said, "How do you know that?"

And the man sputtered, "Why, because I am an engineer!"

Kettering smiled and said, "I'm sure you are. But were you ever a piston in a diesel engine?"

That is the mind-set of a good communicator.

How Genius Destroys Itself

Now and again we employ an alleged genius who is unwilling or unable to live within the minimal disciplines a profit-making institution must have in order to function.

There is probably no way to keep from acquiring one of these erratic humans from time to time, but once his or her work style has been identified as incorrectly structured, you would think that we would have learned to part company quickly. Sadly, we often delay while the damage accumulates.

This kind of person can be one of several types. Some labor incredibly long hours, turning out a prodigious volume of work. Some are very creative with exceptional ability to improvise. Some are warm and engaging and talk apparent sense. The cancerous curse they share, that ultimately devours all they accomplish, is their inability to grasp the most basic principles of record keeping, budget control, expense management, scheduling, deadlines, or promises.

Because they do so many things so well, we try every ploy to focus all their efforts on their strengths and use them in tandem with other, better organized people. It never works and it never will.

Finally, it always develops that some vendor bills are

missing, the time sheets for February are lost, a rent-a-car bill comes in for a trip no one can recall, an estimate is exceeded by 300 percent, the slides for a sales meeting aren't done until 2 A.M. the morning of a meeting that is 700 miles from the slide maker and the airport is fogged in. All the long hours, all the creative brilliance and a ten-year client relationship go down the tube together. And then, for another year, we and our lawyers and accountants try to sort out the messed-up billing and ultimately write off half of the balance as a bad debt. Everybody loses.

It is always tempting to believe that the good the disorganized superstar does will outweigh the dangers and that, given the chance, you can keep things under control.

It won't and you can't.

The Right To Make a Mistake

A lot of what I know—or think I know—is the result of making mistakes.

I've been lucky; I've worked for several people who let me try something they thought probably wouldn't pan out. Often it didn't, but having burned my own hand instead of merely looking at someone else's bandages, the lessons were much easier to remember.

I've learned that one of the hardest things for a manager to do is to preserve for his people the right to make mistakes as a part of their on-the-job training.

The problem is that when a manager sees one of his or her people heading off toward probable danger, there is a point beyond which the risks of calamity become too great. If the actions of the subordinate endanger the whole enterprise, the right to make a mistake becomes too costly. So it can be a tough judgment call for even the most enlightened manager.

From time to time I've rejected promotion plans for clients when I was sure from past experience that they

41

would be totally unacceptable. The account executive has wanted very badly to take them to a client and try to sell them. Sometimes the proposal is so much like a program that was rejected previously that the client will lose confidence in the way we run our business. Sometimes the program is out of phase with the client's style or image. Sometimes it is impractical and costly. Sometimes it is an exercise in creativity, brilliant and engaging, but with low probability of commercial success.

On the other hand, the manager who wants to call all the plays himself never develops self-reliant subordinates. He is the one who fails to train a successor.

The trick is to give people the satisfaction and sometimes the pain of seeing their creations succeed or fail without getting the establishment in trouble. The ability to do so is the single most important trait of management excellence.

The Jacquin Curse

When I was a young man working on a daily newspaper, I had an editor named Eddie Jacquin. I left after five years and he sent me off with a gold watch and the Jacquin Curse.

The watch was stolen from me from a Pittsburgh hotel room years ago but I can't get rid of the Jacquin Curse.

Eddie Jacquin was not so much a great grammarian as he was a clear thinker and therefore a clear writer. He hated redundancies, euphemisms, clichés and verbal bush-beating. So spooked was I by the Jacquin Curse that through all the intervening years certain writing transgressions have the same effect on me as sharp chalk drawn across a blackboard.

And so I can never see a phrase such as "most outstanding" without wincing.

I read that Edwin Newman is irritated by all the evasiveness we use to avoid saying "toilet." Once I reported that the University of Illinois was considering rebuilding the press box atop Memorial Stadium to add restrooms. "Damn it," said Eddie, "write 'toilets.' Do you think that with the score tied, bands playing and 55,000 people screaming their lungs out, anyone is going to a room to rest?"

Once newspaper sports pages were a tangle of cloying clichés, where a team was always a quintet or an eleven or a duo. Nicknames took the place of cities, states and colleges. Only a dedicated buff knew who had beat which and at what. Today the press seems more straightforward but the disease is virulent among radio and television score readers, causing me to cut myself while shaving, even with nick-proof blades. Mr. Jacquin would have done likewise.

I remember once starting a story, "Under azure October skies . . . " and then running on for a couple of paragraphs about the slight chill in the air, the yellow maples in the distance, the smell of burning leaves and hot dogs cooking, all in a coordinated celebration of the football season. It came back to me with a blunt question: "Who the hell won the game?"

I suppose I'd consider it a fine legacy if I could pass the curse along to a new generation as the Marsteller Curse. If I could leave just a few people permanently uncomfortable in the presence of shabby, superficial or untuned writing, I would have left a small mark of which I'd be proud.

And so would Eddie Jacquin.

The Delights of a Deadline

Many, probably most, people hate deadlines. They just don't like to be faced with the fact that at some very specific time, they must have something done.

I love deadlines. In fact, I am now convinced that nearly all successful and contented people need and want deadlines. I believe this so strongly that I never give myself open-ended assignments. If no deadline exists for the completion of a job, I set one.

Working on a newspaper is the greatest discipline there is. Deadlines occur constantly, and everyone works by the same clock. Produce or perish.

Any writer, any artist, any anyone who will live by tough deadlines will get a lot more done. And since one of the most important factors in the development of a skill is practice, it follows that an enormously high percentage of excellent work comes from prolific producers.

Some of the best work we do comes from moving quickly from the heat of ideation to the immediacy of execution. I've sat in many a meeting where dozens of great ideas were harvested and everyone went away excited. But follow-through was postponed for a few days, and other problems intervened. Then, when people got down to the toil of getting the job done, enthusiasm had wilted, memories were blurred, the creative thrust was dulled.

Other times we've done fine things when time was merciless, and the people went from an exciting meeting with the warmth of inspiration right into execution. Working that way, the excitement shines through the finished product.

Nothing much is accomplished by delay. Everything dies a little every day and a creative idea is the most perishable thing I know.

Setting Standards, Following Standards

We confuse ourselves with our image of what excellence is. We tend to think of excellence as a brilliantly executed inspiration.

But this is all wrong. Excellence is not reserved for the inordinately talented; excellence, I am convinced, springs not so much from stark inventiveness as from clarity of purpose and attention to detail.

Creative Management

When you come down to it, running a small company is an intensely personal thing. The kind of company you or I will have will probably be a pretty fair replica of the kind of people we are, and what we want most, and like best and stand for.

*   *   *   *

It is usually said that the agency's first responsibility properly is to its client. This is one of the reasons often given by the commission-system skeptics that the current method of paying agencies is wrong. It is my firm belief that the way the agency is paid has nothing to do with the discharge of its responsibilities to the client because its paramount responsibility is to itself.

The agency that serves its clients best is the one with the principles and courage to be sure that the promotion it prepares and places is honest, in good taste, representative of its best abilities, and is the kind of advertising it would run if it were held fully liable for the success or failure of the plan.

To shift responsibility to the client—to say "we had to do it this way because the client insisted on it"—is a one-way ticket to trouble.

*   *   *   *

Fortunately it is quite possible to be both optimistic and pragmatic. Pragmatism for the short range; optimism for the future. Wars are waged, but they ultimately end.

*   *   *   *

There is the story of the boy's mother who called from the other room, "Marvin, are you spitting in the goldfish bowl?" And Marvin said, "No, but I'm coming pretty close."

Close is a way to describe failure as near success. Close is a synonym for the best in mediocrity; it is a contradiction and in reality cannot be. Close is when you *almost* care enough to want the very best.

46

The Elitism of Excellence

Everyone says that advertising is a people business. So are dentistry, figure skating, cooking, violin soloing, painting and prostitution. So also are surgery, ice hockey, string quartets, professional football, opera and X-rated movies. But the two groups are quite different.

The skills that determine excellence in the first group are not enough for success in the second. There's an extra ingredient needed. Sportswriters call it teamwork. Music critics call it empathy. In some endeavors it is even called love. Whatever, it's rooted in mutual respect, shared objectives and a common drive to be the best. It is a wholesome form of elitism. All successful organizations have this innate sense of their own superiority.

All outstanding organizations develop a momentum of their own. The big get bigger; the rich get richer; the winners roll right on through management changes, retirement and the inevitable blips brought about by momentary complacency. Successful organizations can maintain that momentum indefinitely so long as they hold tight to the principles that made them stand out in the first place. But there will always be some people attracted by the prestige of the successful organization who will attach themselves to it and then pick away at the very practices and policies and beliefs that are the mosaic of its eminence. They must be rudely kicked away if the organization is to keep what it has and build on it for the years to come.

Any company that wants to grow and prosper has got to purge itself of people who can be satisfied with Hershey bars, running water and a subscription to *Penthouse*. There are phonies in this and any other industry and if they infiltrate our ranks we must expose them and expunge them. It is a function of our times that some companies brag about growth while their bills go unpaid. It is a function of the times that there are those who, for a while, are able to camouflage incompetence with arrogance. We must not confuse the real with the imitation.

What is it that develops organizational excellence?

First, of course, is a bone-deep desire to be the best. Not merely as a statement of corporate dogma, but a desire that becomes a part of the heartbeat of all who come to stay and create a career.

Second, it's a great respect for one's self and for each other. If around you there are others whose character and ability and dedication trade at par with your own, that will translate easily into pride—pride in yourself, pride in the group.

Third, it's a commitment to moral and ethical business behavior. But the observance of that commitment is up to the individual. Henry David Thoreau, of all people, wrote: "It is truly enough said that a corporation has no conscience. But a corporation of conscientious men is a corporation with a conscience." The excellent organization can harbor no shortcutters and no maneuverers.

And that suggests a fourth trait that has blessed us and all other coordinated and happy groups—an absence of internal politics. The office politician is a parasite but fortunately easily identified and exterminated.

Finally, excellence is nurtured by the hereditary genes of dissatisfaction. Very little of what we do today is good enough for tomorrow. It's fine to stuff your stomach with the satisfaction of accomplishment so long as you stop in time so that by morning you will be hungry again. When applicants bring me a portfolio of ads they have done, I push them aside and say, "Tell me instead about the ads you expect to do tomorrow."

There are easier places to work than here. It is not a somnambulant life. With losers there is usually a certain lassitude and the rules are lax, but winners are always just a little bit tense and hot to trot. I'm fully aware that some of our newer people think that coming to work on time, dressing properly, treating service people as equals, being on schedule for meetings, keeping clean desks and offices and rewriting and reworking and polishing and rehearsing and being edited and even starting all over again are all intrusions into their lifestyle. Indeed they are and we make no apologies. Here we share a different lifestyle—one that assumes leadership, distinction and respect for the mores of others. You may think these things are petty but they are part of an attitude that says, "We want to be unique—we want to be the best in all ways."

If you are good enough, you can be very happy in a group of achievers, but if you are satisfied with merely passing grades, or if you are consummately self-centered, it is a tough go.

A few years ago, the Marine Corps ran an ad: "We need a few extraordinary recruits for a dangerous mission. Must be five feet, ten inches or over, in perfect health with 20-20 vision uncorrected, courageous and able to withstand extreme physical and mental pressure." Soon thereafter a recruiting sergeant looked up to see a skinny, bald five-footer with a concave chest and thick glasses standing before him holding the ad.

The Marine said, "What the hell do you want?"

The little man handed him the ad. He said, "I just came to tell you: on me you shouldn't count!"

Every day of my working life I see new evidence of what can be accomplished by organizations made up of people who respect themselves individually and collectively.

A company is, after all, only a confederation of individuals. It takes its shape from the composite character of the people it hires and keeps.

If it attracts cynics, it becomes a bilious organism with lines around the mouth and gas on the stomach.

If it attracts drones who work there only because they have to work somewhere, it becomes a nine-to-five citadel of aimlessness and boredom.

If it attracts sharpies and social trespassers, it will attract that kind of client and is doomed to live a furtive existence in the shadows of uncertainty.

But, if it attracts people with self-set and self-maintained standards of excellence, there is nothing it can be denied.

Certain Inalienable Rights

If you came to work for our company, you acquired certain uncancellable rights, among them:

- The right to be treated fairly and courteously, and with respect for your individual dignity.
- The right to know where you stand—how your performance is rated by your managers. Our policy is that everyone should be given a proper performance evaluation at least once a year, and if you haven't, you have the right to insist on it.
- The right to your own religious, political and social beliefs without jeopardy to your job.
- The right to expect this company to conduct our business ethically and honestly at all times.
- The right to guidance and support in your own program of occupational self-development.
- The right to take a grievance to any level of management without threat or fear of recrimination.

If you came to work here, you also acquired certain responsibilities—certain basic policies and principles we expect of everyone as a condition of employment.

- The obligation to be fair and courteous to everyone with whom you work, for whom you work, or who works for you. In short, the obligation to be a gentleman or gentlewoman.
- Honesty and truthfulness in your relationships with clients, with the company, and with each other.
- Being at work on time. Consistently.
- Keeping your work area neat and clean. Always.
- The obligation not to impose your personal beliefs on others.

These rights and obligations are universal. They apply to everyone regardless of location, job category, sex, color, or nationality, or length of service.

In any organization as large and widespread as ours, almost certainly there will be some who will deliberately or inadvertently work at cross-purposes to these principles. There will also be cases where two people may have two interpretations of a given happening.

But these are the ground rules for employment with us and we are dedicated to maintaining them. How well we are able to do so, of course, depends not on company policy but upon their acceptance by the individuals who in the aggregate constitute the company. The same as anywhere else.

The Day That Marilyn Dropped In*

A soft, insinuating, love-laden voice said, "Am I intruding?"

I looked up from my desk and nearly slid to the floor. Standing there, more glamorous than in any picture, was America's sex goddess, Marilyn Monroe.

Her soft, blonde hair, hanging loosely to her shoulders, shimmered in the sun. Her eyes were deep and clear and somehow sympathetic and understanding. Her full red lips were parted just slightly, almost as if inside she was panting with excitement. Her yellow-gold knit dress was form-tight, clearly outlining her high, firm bosom, her flat stomach, her esquisitely rounded hips, and her splendidly symmetrical thighs.

I recovered, only enough to ask, "Won't you sit down?"

She crossed her legs, and then I noticed.

Instead of stockings, whe was wearing ankle socks that came up only two inches above her shoes. Above them, her legs were covered with a thick, matted growth of black hair.

I threw up in the waste basket.

---

*From "The Wonderful World of Words"

Creative Management

Now fellas, if Marilyn Monroe can't get away with it, how come you think you can?

And shaving your legs won't help much either. Even those of you who ain't so hairy tend to have awfully white legs, often with goose bumps.

Very few companies, in my opinion, have more people with good looking legs than this company, but they are all on girls.

I have the feeling that our clients aren't knocked out with our legs either.

Perhaps I'm getting old, but I'm getting more conscious of men's legs between the tops of these silly little ankle socks and the high rise of trousers when seated. It's sloppy and unbusinesslike. You don't need to wear garters to avoid it. At all price ranges, there now are socks on the market at various lengths that stay up without garters, even on skinny legs. I know.

Are you still with me?

If so, on to the next problem.

Sports jackets.

When we open our office in Waterloo, Iowa, all the staff ought to wear them every day. Everybody in Waterloo does. When in Waterloo, do as the Waterloons.

But take New York or Chicago, for instance.

If you're in the office all day, OK. But, generally, if you are going to be out, calling on clients, or you are going to have outsiders calling on you, wear a suit, huh?

You can tell me some of our clients wear sports jackets to work.

All I know is I never saw the head of a single client company in a big city in a sports jacket in the office.

I would also add that they mostly have clean finger-nails, but they never seem to work on them in my presence.

As far as I know, they have clean noses, but I don't recall any of them picking them in a conference.

And I expect they itch as much as you do sometimes, but if they scratch in public, they're pretty sneaky about it.

You still here?

OK, then about smoking.

I smoke. I don't intend to quit.

But some people don't like smoking in their offices. And some people don't like cigars or pipes at all.

So I never, never light up in a stranger's office unless and until he does. And I never smoke a pipe or cigar unless there is evidence he does.

I know you wouldn't do that either, so I probably shouldn't even bring it up.

Never, never, never smoke during a presentation, inside or out. No smokes on the podium.

Now:

Do I do something I ought to know about?

Write me.

Anonymously, of course.

Alexander Graham Pompous

This morning I called the newly appointed vice president of sales of one of the country's largest publishing firms to invite him to lunch. I dialed the call myself, as I always do.

His secretary answered, "Mr. Shirt's Office."

"This is Bill Marsteller. Is Mr. Shirt in?"

"What did you say your name was?"

"Bill Marsteller. It not only was; it still is."

"How do you spell it?"

"M-A-R-S-T-E-L-L-E-R. Is Mr. Shirt in?"

"What company are you with, Mr. Marsteller?"

"Marsteller, Incorporated. Is Mr. Shirt in?"

"Is that the advertising agency?"

"Yes. Now Miss—"

"Mr. Shirt has someone with him. May I tell him what this is about?"

"Look, Miss, just have him call me, please. 752-6500."

Time passes. The phone rings. I answer. "Bill Marsteller."

"Mr. Stuffed Shirt is calling Mr. Marsteller."

"This is Mr. Marsteller."

"Will you hold please for Mr. Shirt."

Time passes. I read the *Wall Street Journal* and finish *Gone With The Wind*.

Finally, "Bill? Stuffed here. What can I do for you?"

Shall I tell him? No—it's a waste of time.

"Sorry," I say. "I've forgotten why I called you. If it ever occurs to me I'll write a letter." Possibly to his president.

We have some policies that bear on this:

- If you're in your office and not in a meeting, answer your own phone.
- No secretary in this outfit asks a caller to state his business.
- Best you should place your own calls, but if you don't, pick up *immediately* when the person you are calling answers.
- Be sure your telephone is covered when you are away from your desk.
- Answer unattended ringing phones and offer to take a message.
- Don't get caught up in your own importance. A pompous ass has no class.

Do Clothes Make the Man?*

Of course not, although it is widely believed they sometimes make the woman. They don't even successfully disguise the man for long.

You can dress eccentric as hell, but if you can only look and act eccentric, your commercial value will soon be established as negative.

I keep interviewing alleged creative people and I'll tell

---

*From "The Wonderful World of Words."

you that a lot of these wild rags are just a security blanket. A good creative person doesn't have to look like he, she or it was conceived in the exhaust pipe of a motorcycle.

If your ambition is to get a lot of your things approved by the client, you've either got to leave that to the comb and brush crowd or strike some bourgeois compromise yourself. You know, sell out to the system like Bill Bernbach or Mary Wells.

None of which is to say that a white shirt and a crew cut is any good as a disguise if down deep you're shallow. A blue serge suit doesn't beget dependability. There are a lot of recorded cases where a vice president who dressed like Herbert Hoover took off with Myrtle, the teller in cage No. 3, along with a duffel bag packed with a lavender and pink sport shirt and $206,431 worth of the stuff he was watching for widows and orphans.

There may be some kind of satisfaction in being way head of or way behind the norm of the place and time. But those satisfactions are Mickey Mouse compared to the satisfactions of moving people, of getting things printed or spieled.

There is, as the liquor people always tell you correctly if not always convincingly, a happy medium.

Just remember, the freak show is never in the main tent.

Reaffirmation of Faith, Supplier Division

Of late, I've spend mucho hours reviewing our supplier situation.

And their are problems. So, folks, let's reexamine our principles and get the establishment tuned up again.

First, we do not wish to proliferate suppliers. We want to concentrate our business with very few, work very closely with them, and deal with principals, not salesmen or brokers. What suppliers would pay salesmen should be used to reduce prices to us and our clients.

Second, we do not accept presents from suppliers. Anyone who does will get his or her butt, however cute or gross, kicked out into the street. OK for lunches, or if they send out cranberries or even a bottle of schnapps for Yule. But that's it.

Third, we always issue purchase orders. Not mostly. Always.

Fourth, we must have up-to-date data on the financial status of all suppliers.

Fifth, we don't buy from your brother-in-law. If he's lucky enough to be in your family, that's reward enough.

We want suppliers who will be dedicated to us. Us is the company. Not an individual.

And, if they do good work, on time and at a competitive price, we intend to be dedicated to them.

In Defense of Company Policies

We have just distributed to all employees an updated recapitulation of our policies.

The receipt of a new handbook of company policy is likely to be greeted with the degree of enthusiam normally reserved for the receipt of a bill for unpaid taxes. However, all companies have policies whether they are published or are communicated by rumor. In the infinite wisdom of management, we have concluded that our associates would prefer to have our particular brand of principles set forth in a handy document that can be referred to from time to time as the game progresses.

Now for some pompous profundities about these simply smashing edicts.

First, nearly all of them came about because of error, misunderstanding, noses out of joint, government fiat, miscarriage of justice, or Dire Disaster. In other words, they came into being as an attempt to avoid committing the same mistakes repeatedly. Which is to say that having discovered that playing with matches frequently results in unwanted fires, we rule out the avocational use of matches before the whole place burns down.

Then there are the policies aimed at maintaining a consistent and consistently high corporate code of conduct. It is clearly our right and duty to decide the standards of company behavior and then to require individual adherence to them. When one bird fouls the nest, the smell clings to all that roost there.

Also there are the policies of democracy. These are the directives that rest on Abraham Lincoln's proposition that all men are created equal. They say, in one way or another: I will not ask you to do what I am unwilling to do; you have no right to ask of me that which you are unwilling to give in return; your fundamental rights and mine are interchangeable.

Because our policies are not the prejudices of any one person, it has taken 18 months to revise, clarify and minimize them.

What is left is an imperfect set of regulations, objectives, strivings and concepts intended to reduce the number of instances where the answer is, "I didn't know what was expected."

Policies should be set in type but not cement. People change, society changes, laws change, goals change, and so policies must change. Those we have just published are no doubt already in transition. But unless we make policy changes for good and considered reasons, the company also changes, and the understanding that held it together is lost.

31 People Who Didn't Do So Well Here

1. There was the guy who asked me, "How much money would I need to start my own agency?"

2. There was the poor fellow whose wife called me twice to explain that her husband should have been promoted instead of someone else.
3. There was the girl who came to work with a bare midriff.
4. There was the girl who ran around the office in her bare feet and diapered her baby in the reception room (though she did later become rich and famous as a folk singer).
5. There was the manager who brought his moods to the office and spread them around like the common cold.
6. And the manager whose hobby was gossip.
7. And the manager who reacted to confidential information like most people react to raw vegetables and tap water in Mexico.
8. Then there was the lady who came in 20 minutes late all the time even though she lived within easy walking distance of the office.
9. And the dum-dum who put in an expense account for a classy dinner and theater tickets for a client who that week happened to be with me in Florida.
10. And the doting father who kept his kids in pencils, scratch pads, marking pens, paper clips, staples, and art supplies out of our stock room.
11. Then there was the copywriter who moonlighted for another agency writing on an account competitive to one of ours.
12. There was the guy who called big think-tank meetings and always came late, if at all, and left early, hardly noticed.
13. There was this bird who went on and on about how great it was at the company where he used to work.
14. There was this self-designated hotshot who had no time and no courtesy for switchboard operators, secretaries, production people, mail room personnel, and the like, who was finally exposed as a stuffy fraud by switchboard operators, secretaries, production people, mail room personnel, and the like. He has finally taken up an

occupation more in keeping with his character: He is a proctologist for horses.
15. And then there were the other 17 men and women exactly like him who got the shaft in exactly the same way.

The End of Loose Living

In grammar school, I hated arithmetic. In high school, I slogged through the required three years of algebra and geometry without ever fully understanding what was going on. In college, I conned the management into letting me substitute psychology and geography for the mathematics requirement.

I am not, therefore, an hereditary aficionado of billing details, expense accounts, budgets, production estimates, time sheets, conference reports, and other impedimenta that stand in the way of the casual life.

Long ago, however, I painfully concluded that disdain of or indolence toward these details lead inevitably to various predictable disasters such as customer outrage, unbillable write-offs, the massive wasting of other people's time and atrophied profits.

I have never used my position on the corporate letterhead to ask others to do unpleasant tasks that I avoid. Therefore, with clear conscience and the zeal of the converted sinner, I have reminded one and all that egotistical hotshots (like me) are not exempt from the drek work that is the physiological curse of business—periodic and irreversible.

No one is so creative, no one is so beloved, no one is so hard working that he or she can flaunt the system, which is as minimal as we can make it and still maintain a healthy business. We have no corporate pride in the size of our record keeping and accounting function; in fact it is the detail deviates among us who proliferate the very function they seemingly wish to ignore.

I am aware of the company-wide conspiracy to let me hear only good news. However, long ago I discovered a remarkable law-giver named Murphy who said that if everything is going well, it is obvious that you have over-looked something. Tracing those accounting problems that *do* come to my attention, I invariably find one or both of two basic causes:

Carelessness, and assumption that others would do the follow-up; or excessive self-adoration that developed an attitude that one's own brilliance exempted him or her from the constraints of mere mortals.

No prudent company can afford either.

Manners for the Maladroit

Among the rebellious, there are probably a goodly number of people who practice bad manners as an ignorant form of social protest.

Most of us, however, are guilty of bad manners acci-dentally, usually because of insensitivity to our own habits. None of us is without some bits of boorishness that grate on others. With that wind-up, I will now deliver some lapses in gentility that bother me.

I am annoyed by:

- People you haven't seen for a long time (if ever) who say, "You don't remember me, do you?"
- People who put out cigarettes on their dinner plate. Or lunch plate.
- People too insecure or too self-imporant ever to answer their own phone.
- People too insecure or too self-important ever to place their own phone calls.

- People who put their feet on their desk and in your face when talking to you.
- People who smoke while speaking before a group.
- People who chew gum while speaking before a group.
- People who won't order a meal until they find out what you are having.
- People who are always late for meetings.
- People who paste things on office walls.
- People who don't flush.
- People who put drink glasses down without coasters.
- People who leave closet doors open.
- People who barge into your office while you're on the phone and just stand there looking impatient.

Hiring, Firing and Retiring

We want achievers; failure is uncomfortable in the presence of success. In a world so concerned for the underdog, I honor the upperdog—the doer, the succeeder. There can be no great society (or company) unless individual achievement is encouraged.

Creative Management

Pruning—cutting away the weak limbs so that there's more room and more light for the strong ones to grow—is one of the hardest jobs in any business.

We hire a man or woman with hope, persecute him with procrastination, and fire him with fear. And it's wrong—it's bad business and immoral.

Unfortunately, ineptitude is as contagious as excellence and, just as your brightest people polish everyone to some degree, so does the friction of contact with your dullest people, just a little, erode the strength of everyone with whom they work.

*   *   *   *

Most performance evaluation programs fail because managers hate face-to-face appraisal. They are more embarrassed than the employee being evaluated. Many employee terminations are surprises to the one being severed because someone was too ill-at-ease to tell the truth.

*   *   *   *

The next matter I wish to clear up is indispensability. Years ago when I had to absent myself from a board of directors meeting for an hour or so, one of our directors said, "This is a good time to bring up a problem I know has troubled many of us. To wit: What are we going to do if Bill Marsteller dies?" The guy who was at that time the manager of our Chicago office said, "I think we ought to bury the son-of-a-bitch." So much for indispensability. So much also for the manager of the Chicago office.

*   *   *   *

I hope that the overdue push for equal opportunity and reward for women doesn't destroy the tradition that women make better secretaries, because they absolutely do. It has nothing to do with who makes the coffee. I can make my own breakfast, but I can't begin to match the priceless combination of tact, charm, technical skills, devotion and judgment that makes a great secretary.

This may get me in trouble, but I think women's lib is often too concerned with getting women out of traditional women's jobs. A better and more balanced and more useful approach is to seek to upgrade both the job and the job holder—in status, job satisfaction, responsibility, pay and importance.

Hiring Without Tests or Tears

When I got out of college in 1937, advertising agencies simply didn't hire trainees, and newspapering, which had gotten me through school, did not pay a decent wage.

I wound up working for the Massachusetts Mutual Life Insurance Company. Several insurance companies were dabbling in methods to select agents a little more scientifically than through kidnapping and bribery, and I was sent to a seminar to learn how to give aptitude tests.

In 1941 when I left the Mass, the vastly relieved management gave me a farewell dinner. In the midst of it, a telegram was delivered to me. It read: "We knew you'd finally take that damned test yourself." It was signed by 41 people whom I had selected as excellent prospects for success but who had all failed badly, frequently owing the company a sizable amount for advances against sales they never made.

Experiences of that sort early in life tend to leave suture marks. So my normal open-minded liberal point of view does not extend to routine aptitude testing.

On the other hand, I am appalled at how casual and primitive some hiring is. Following a few sensible steps without deviation, whether you're hiring a new college graduate or an account supervisor, will greatly reduce the failure ratio.

- Never hire without interviewing four or five people for the same job so that you have a basis for comparison.
- Never hire unless at least two others have also interviewed the prospect and you have their ratings.
- Never hire until you've had at least two separate interviews with the prospect.
- Never hire in a hurry. Allow some days for your first enthusiasm to cool.
- Always check references and insist on talking with former employers or teachers—several of

them. Write out the questions you intend to ask—don't wing it. Not general questions, but questions like, "What happens when he has three things to do at once? What kind of people does he impress most? Is he old or young for his age? What was the best thing he ever did for you?" That's how you find things out; not by just asking is he honest, sober and normal in the noggin. Also, talk to the prospect's contemporaries, if possible.

- Ask every prospective employee what he expects to be doing ten years from now. Stay with it; force answers. Ask how he expects to get there.

Behind the Job Hunting Facade

Most managers, when they're interviewing prospective new employees, ask questions like "Are you honest? Do you drink to excess? did you get good grades in school? Why did you leave your last job?"

Such a waste of time. Do you expect someone to admit being a dumb alcoholic thief who got canned for incompetence and sloth?

Good interviewing combines an element of surprise with some off-beat questions that probe beyond the obvious.

Here are some I use:

- If you come to work here, what do you expect to be doing in five years? In 20 years?
- What did you do last Saturday and Sunday? Take me through those days.
- What do you most admire about your wife (husband, tentmate)?
- In your opinion, what's the best museum in town? Why?

- What were the last two books you've read?
- Who are your two closest friends? Tell me about them.
- Here's paper and pencil. Take five minutes to write down the adjectives that best describe you.
- What school would you rather have gone to than the one you did? Why?
- What do you think the economic situation will be a year from today?
- If you could just get in a car and drive for 30 days, where would you go?
- What's the greatest honor you've ever had?
- What did you learn from the last person you worked for on how to get along with people?
- What would you hope your children would do when they're grown?
- Can you type?
- What television programs interest you most?
- Of all the people you've been associated with, whom did you dislike most? Why?
- What do you remember most happily from your childhood?
- If you were me, why would you hire you?

Now, aren't you glad I didn't interview you?

Homegrown vs. Processed

My attitude toward employment agencies is about the same as it is toward escort services: If you have to use them, you didn't do something right. And a corollary caution: Don't expect unblemished merchandise.

Now I'm sure there are some fine, high-quality employment agencies but not so many as to justify a special heading in the Yellow Pages. In my experience, most employment agencies have done more harm than good. In the process of keeping fees flowing, they artificially drive up salaries, breed vocational discontent, promote egocentricity, peddle mediocrity and create damaged careers. Almost never will they tell someone to stay put. Almost never will they suggest to a prospect that perhaps he or she is fairly paid, or that his or her qualifications are limited, or that job-hopping is not a by-pass around traffic on the road to the Holy Grail.

This outburst is the result of once again interviewing a platoon of employment agency referrals. You see, we don't always do things right either and wind up calling the agencies to send over some samples. Half of those I've seen act like shuttlecocks from a three-hour badminton game, which is to say batted around. A few tell me they are so brilliant I don't think we could live up to their standards.

Let me explain that for clerical workers, some employment agencies perform a useful service, but only if they operate merely as conduits, not salespeople. Also, for specialized, high-level executives, there are some excellent search firms. But whenever we have used one I have felt we failed along the way.

The solution is a constant program of recruiting, training, evaluation. It is expensive, but in the end it is less costly than the aggregate fees paid for trial-and-error hiring of someone else's discontended wanderers.

I'll take the homegrown instead of the processed whenever there's a choice. If you develop your own, you'll know about weaknesses as well as strengths. You will have made your impact on work habits, ethical beliefs, style and loyalty.

The difficulty with this approach is you must institute it far in advance of need. You have to believe and you have to be patient. But oh the rewards! It is not just a coincidence that the people who run IBM and Procter & Gamble and General Foods and General Motors and, I am proud to say, Marsteller and Burson-Marsteller, came a long time ago, came to stay, and came to succeed.

Notes From a Male Chauvinist Pussy-Cat

Most mail surveys (except, of course, those conceived on our premises) are pretty dumb. The one I got the other day asking about our employment policies with respect to the "professional woman" is a case in point.

First, I have to say about the professional woman that I have never met an amateur woman.

With all seriousness, however, attitudes toward women are finally changing, and we are making a serious effort to lead, not simply reluctantly follow.

In our recruiting, we are hiring many more women than just a few years ago. The reason, however, is not simply or even mainly social consciousness. Rather it's because we are finding that nowadays so many of the best graduates of journalism and advertising courses are women.

Ten years ago, we had one woman officer and two women department heads. As this is written we have 11 women officers, 22 women department heads, and 56 more in assignments that I guess would be classified as "professional."

I have written to the several clubs to which I belong urging that their musty main dining rooms be liberated, so all our people, regardless of sex, can share equally in the bad food.

We deserve no praise for these small steps. They all represent enlightened self-interest. There are just too many supremely able women to overlook this source of personnel excellence.

One of my principal extracurricular activities is serving as a trustee of a great women's college. We are bombarded by demands for recognition of women—many of them valid, some frivolous, some unwisely arbitrary. I am, for instance, amused that some of the same women who want all men off the board of trustees (we are a feeble minority) want more men in the dorms and showers. But I suppose that that, too, is enlightened self-interest.

We have no male-female quotas for hiring or promotion in our company. I guess we simply want to be the best and it is increasingly evident that one of the surest ways to be best is to be certain that there is true equality of opportunity.

The Joys of Youth

One of the nicest things about corporate growth and success is that you can afford to have more young people around.

Once upon a time almost everyone who worked in our company was young, even—the legend to the contrary—me. At the time we thought being young was something of a nuisance because most of the corporate people who were our prime prospects were much older and not entirely comfortable with us.

But we kept plugging away and finally solved the problem—we got older. Not wiser, necessarily, and certainly not more energetic—just older. I knew I was older when I could finally afford a funky convertible and found out it was too late for it to do a thing for me.

The young people coming into the company today are fantastic. Not only in the United States, but abroad. One of our officers is just back from two weeks in Europe, having eaten his way through clients, and he says the thing that impressed him most was the ability and poise of our quite young account and creative people. In London, for instance, our growth is being stoked by, and our excellent product created by, a group almost entirely under 30 years old.

Our obligation to these young men and women throughout the company is a bit awesome. We've got to work hard at giving them more repsonsibility faster. We must give them freedom to make some mistakes, for learning comes at least as much from failure as success. We must include them in, take them along, listen to them, treat them as individuals with different degrees of maturity, different goals, different strengths and deficiencies. Most of all we probably should quit referring to them as "trainees" and certainly must quit thinking of them that way.

I discovered the other day that our average age, overall, has actually gone down in the last two years, and since so far as I know no senior officer has discovered an old family Bible that reestablishes his age as less than had been previously claimed, it seems clear that we are blessing ourselves with the joy of youth.

And that is a kind of corporate insurance Prudential doesn't write.

The Worst Job

The rottenest part of a manager's job is firing someone.

If it's some slob who is goofing off or has been spitting on customers in public, it's not so bad. But that is very seldom the situation. Usually it's just a case of persistent sub-par performance, usually beyond the control of the firee.

Because it's such an unpleasant activity, a lot of companies gradually stack up deadwood, with two debilitating results. First, it slowly lowers the standard of work being turned out by the company. Second, it keeps all the chairs filled and therefore discourages hiring bright, motivated new people.

No company wants to get a reputation for personnel ruthlessness, but between that and the mold of mass mediocrity is a happy medium.

Ineptitude is as contagious as excellence and strong management must accept careful pruning as a necessary part of the cultivation of corporate success. It is urgent that the weak limbs be cut away so that there's more room and more light for the strong ones to grow.

If, after we've honestly tried, we can't make a long-range job and future for an employee, we should have the courage to face him with the facts. In the long run, we'll both be better off.

Tell All*

Sometime during the 1930s, during a period when Franklin D. Roosevelt used businessmen for logs for his fireside chats, the "tell all" theory of employee communications was born.

During this time, when business was widely pictured as a vast conspiracy to subjugate the American working class, businessmen began programs to inform their employees of all kinds of inner workings of their companies. Unfortunately, most employees were improperly prepared to deal with all this information. A statement that Company X was seeking a new bank loan was assumed to be an indication of coming bankruptcy. An announcement that a company was going to build a plant addition caused consternation because employees, far from interpreting it as a positive move, saw it as a prelude to new technolgies with which they were unfamiliar and preferred to so remain.

Anyway, after 15 years or so, *Fortune* ran a series on the perils of corporate overcommunication.

Some of our management have been recently troubled by this old communications problem. What should you tell the troops about what the management is up to?

For instance:

We recently dismissed an account executive. We made no public announcement of this always unpleasant action, not wanting to hurt the man and not being particularly proud of guessing wrong in hiring him. He, however, did

---

*From "The Wonderful World of Words."

not go quietly. He made the rounds of a number of offices telling his associates how poorly he had been treated, how little notice he had been given, how we were on the verge of losing at least one of the accounts upon which he had toiled, and how he had been given absolutely no reason for the discharge, and how, some Friday, it will happen to you.

At a recent management meeting, we discussed whether we should perhaps send out notices to folks around the house when something like this happens so that people can judge the facts more fairly.

Therefore, I have prepared a prototype release for the next such case, with the facts based on the last one.

Effective at five o'clock Friday, John Jones is being fired as account executive in our New York office.

He was hired seven months ago after being interviewed by three people. Two of the three had doubts at the time, but he showed such good samples and his last boss praised him so highly that we decided to take a chance.

Unfortunately, it developed that his samples were done by others and his reference was good largely because his last company was anxious to avoid a long unemployment insurance claim.

It developed he simply could not meet our standards, as to either quality or quantity. Further, one of our clients reported that the man had made disparaging remarks about both his supervisor and our company. We found this not difficult to believe since he constantly made disparaging remarks about the client to us.

He has had two employee evaluations and has been told in short, simple words that his work was unsatisfactory. He had read his own employee evaluation and thanked his supervisor for being so frank and helpful. However, his attitude will likely be quite different on Friday afternoon.

To minimize account handling difficulties, we

have told the clients on whose accounts he has been working that he is to be replaced. One said: "I don't recall him." The other said: "Thank God!"

Naturally we wish him well and want to do everything we can to help him get another job.

Blessed Be the Tie that Binds

I have little patience with some of the traditional rites of employee termination. When someone quits, there is often a rustling around to throw a party for him or her. I decline all such invitations and discourage the use of company funds for any such affairs. Not because of sour stomach or a rusted purse, but if I'm going to spend time or money on parties, I think they should be for people who stay, not people who go.

As long as it was easy to do, wherever I went I took as many of our able, loyal people to lunch as I could, for no reason at all other than the fact that they deserved recognition and appreciation. But in 25 years I could count on my fingers the number of ex-employees I've taken to lunch. Ex-employees don't charge me up very much unless and until they are re-employed here.

Most ex-employees are boring. They spend their time with you flexing the facts about their salary, working conditions and opportunities, trying to justify their defection when of course no justification is needed or wanted except, perhaps, by themselves.

Now and again someone who used to labor here drops in to see me. It is reported that I often seem to be annoyed with them. Not so; I'm usually just not very turned on.

Each of us is capable of just so much interest in, concern for and love of our fellow man. I choose to spend mine on the people who are here, not those who have signed on elsewhere. As far as I'm concerned, this is where it's at.

The Charlie Brower Prescription

When Charlie Brower was about to retire as president of BBDO in 1970, he issued an epistle that distilled what he had learned in his lengthly, distinguished, and happy career.

I have held tightly to a copy of it because I agreed with what he said and loved the way he said it. Also, I thought that when I got ready to retire and people came knocking on my door asking for my success prescription, I could pull out Charlie's memo and save a bit of original thinking.

I have been staying close to my office lately listening for knocks, but the only one knocking has been a decorator measuring for new carpet for the next inhabitant. I asked him if he would like some advice, but he looked at my furnishings and said thanks anyway. Young people, whose names I can't seem to remember, hurry by, clearly afraid that if they pause they'll be trapped in an obsolete century.

You can't get away so easily. Avoiding my wisdom is one thing, but I intend to expose you to Charlie Brower's whether you need it or not. This, then, is what he said when he was in a similar fix:

Beside me as I write this is an application blank made to the Columbia University Summer Session in 1926.

Under the question of "Why? etc." I had answered, "I wish to pursue a career in advertising." I have indeed pursued it, and occasionally damned near caught up with it.

The only thing I have found bad about advertising or BBDO is that someday, if you don't get your coronary in time, you have to leave. In my case, it will be the end of this year.

It seems a bit ungracious to just creep away without at least giving my friends a chance to ignore my advice. so here are 16 things I have learned in those 43 years.

- Honesty is not only the best policy, it is rare enough today to make you pleasantly conspicuous.
- The expedient thing and the right thing are seldom the same thing.
- The best way to get credit is to try to give it away.
- You cannot sink someone else's end of the boat and still keep your own afloat.
- If you get a kick out of your job, others will get a kick out of working for you.
- It is not important that you come in early and work late. The important thing is *why?*
- No one should knock research who has ever been helped by a road map.
- Chicken Little acted before her research was complete. The competition ate her up.
- A writer who can't take it had better win in the first round. (Unfortunately, very little advertising is okayed in the first round.)
- There has never been such a thing as a bad client, as long as he paid his bills.
- A man of stature has no need of status.
- Never trust a man who is Dr. Jekyll to those above him and Mr. Hyde to those under him.
- There are fewer low-interest products than low-interest writers.
- You learn more from your defeats than from your victories.
- Few people are successful unless a lot of other people want them to be.
- Many people know how to make a good living. Few know what to do with it when they have it made.

I have enjoyed BBDO. It has certainly exposed me to what Oliver Wendell Holmes called "The passion and action of your time."

The real reason that I am leaving is that Jim Schule promised to tell me if I began to lose my buttons. Jim went and left me. And I begin to suspect that a couple of those buttons are coming loose.

I have loved it here. I hope you do, too.

Other Assorted Elements of Running Things

The success of a business is in the hands of the buyer, but failure is in the hands of the seller.

Creative Management

In the long run, it profits you far more to sell your product on its *value* rather than on its *price*.

Perhaps the main reason more manufacturers do not sell on value rather than on price is that selling on value is far more difficult than selling on price. It requires, of course, a product that *has* value. But that is only the beginning.

It also requires the marketing wisdom to know what specific "character" you should create for your product to separate it most favorably from all others of its kind. Then it requires the creative skill to crystallize that character on paper or on the air waves and project it into the minds of the right people at the right time.

It requires something else, too—the lonely courage to stand out from the crowd, to tell your own story consistently, year in and year out, regardless of the opportunistic tactics of competition. Perhaps this is the rarest quality of all. It is sometimes called Leadership.

* * * *

Going into our new fiscal year, we will be making tough budgets. There will be some pinching here and there. I expect some bleats of anguish.

When we've had to take a hard line in the past, there's been some grumbling in the ranks that we're cutting off our nose to spite our face, or robbing Peter to pay Paul, or similar creative observations.

Not so. We're doing plastic nose surgery to save our face, or asking Peter to pull up his socks so we can keep on paying him. Paul we probably just won't hire at all.

I am a trustee of three nonprofit organizations. I have no intention of becoming chairman of a fourth.

* * * *

Account losses are either forgivable or unforgivable. Unforgivable is when we are guilty of inattention, carelessness, or the creativity of clods. Forgivable is when the client is a bully, a cheapskate, a twit or a twerp, and after three wonderful decades in this business, I can testify under oath that only one and one-half clients out of one hundred are any of those. When I hear an account departure explained away by damning the client, I bend over and sniff a little

80

because I am very suspicious that the cat-sand being spread around is cover for a malodorous deposit dropped there by the sand-kicker himself. In client/agency relations, the records show a clear correlation between negligence and divorce.

* * * *

The agency of the future will have to provide a better career challenge to greatly reduce the tradition of job hopping in consulting businesses. That means that the large agency that can move ambitious, intelligent young people from assignment to assignment, so that they can keep growing without leaving for another company simply for new experience, will have a big advantage.

* * * *

We've had good experience by using consultants for many non-creative management and administrative jobs. Our basic budget system was set up by a professor of business administration, and he continues his quarterly review of our performance. We've used all kinds of consultants for all kinds of research. This has held down fixed costs, given us merchandisable names, and greatly reduced the time the principals have had to spend on methodology and research procurement. When we've expanded or rented new offices, we've usually used consultants to minimize executive involvement. When we have needed a head-candler or a fashion expert, we have rented them until we were big enough to own our own.

* * * *

Make your open door policy figurative not literal until you get big enough to afford someone who can sit around with his door open and his couch dusted, inviting interruptions. Doors, we tell our people, were made to be closed, so that people can be alone, doing things that people do best alone, like thinking, writing or drawing. There is this crazy idea abroad in business today that you only shut the door when you are firing someone or playing jiggery-pokey with the books. Anybody who has invention as a part of his job description is entitled to periods of rigid non-interruption and isolation.

Creative Management

Several of us used to work with a hard-nosed Rockwell executive named L. A. Dixon. I once attended a Rockwell management meeting called to discuss the unfavorable cost-profit relationships in several divisions.

Someone suggested giving a prize to any division manager who reduced expenses 10 percent.

"That's a helluva idea," Dix said. "The prize should be that anyone who cuts costs 10 percent gets to keep his job. Anyone who don't gets honorable mention which we'll write on his record the same day we kick his ass out of here."

Dix was of the old school and had difficulty adjusting to the more cultivated relationships of these days, but his philosophies of management had a way of working out surprisingly well in many cases.

"I don't need help figuring out ways to spend money," he used to say. "My wife taught me that years ago without getting an MBA degree. What I want from these hotshot managers are ways to do more business at less cost. Any lazy bastard can rent more space or raise salaries or hire a consultant, but you got to think hard to get more out of what you already got."

I remember walking with Dix through a Rockwell plant that had a poor productivity record. At the end of the afternoon, Dix told the plant manager six things to do to get improved labor utilization.

"Tell the foremen to knock it off with the white shirts. They ought to wear work clothes like their men, and when there's a machine breakdown, they'll help fix it instead of standing around squeezing pimples.

"No more reserved parking places. The people who get here first get the best spots. Whoever they are.

"Put a scrap bin by every machine and only pick up scrap just before the end of the shift so everybody can see who's messing up and who isn't.

"Get rid of those big tables in the lunch room. No more than four seats at a table and people won't sit around so long.

"Get rid of departmental bulletin boards. Put 'em between the time clocks and the plant exits. If you got something everybody is supposed to read, hand it out at the door at the end of a shift.

"And turn down the temperature in the toilets and have somebody pick up the newspapers and magazines laying around in there three or four times a day. We ain't running no library."

Silly, you say? Well, Dix ran very efficient plants with darn good morale and loyalty. He wasn't afraid to remind people what they were there for.

You'll note that none of these moves costs money.

As Dix said, no great training is needed to find ways to spend money.

But courageous and creative management is needed to find ways not to spend it.

The Trade-Offs of Management

At the risk of insulting your obvious intelligence, first let me remind you that a company's gross income is the sum total of sales, fees, commissions, markups, discounts earned and retained, interest earned, and perhaps a few other minor items such as the occasional sale of a secondhand water cooler.

And net operating profit is what is left after deducting all the costs of doing business, such as salaries, rent, light, heat, purchases of all kinds, travel, entertainment, insurance, lawyers, auditors, and on and on and on.

In the area of costs, there are continuous management decisions to be made on trade-offs.

Do you wish for more elaborate offices and more space? Well, are you willing to (and can you) cut salary costs enough to offset increased occupancy costs?

Do you want to increase salaries (and therefore all fringe benefit costs)? Are you prepared to squeeze more people into less space?

Creative Management

These are merely two of the most apparent and larger trade-offs. There are dozens of possible combinations, however.

If you want my opinion (which many of you no doubt yearn for with the same fervor you regard parsnips), I think there are certain guidelines established by our experience and that of the best-run competitive businesses.

- Very high salaries will not buy you better people, but on the contrary often attract highly self-oriented people who will not help you build the business and will jump ship when temptation beckons if, indeed, you haven't already pushed them overboard. However, low salaries will not buy good people. People who are interested and challenged will work hard and stay aboard so long as their salaries are competitive with industry standards.
- Expensive offices have an inverse relationship to success in many businesses. For years Doyle Dane Bernbach operated Camelot from some of the least distinguished offices in New York. Customers and clients are suspicious of splendor. High rents and lush surroundings create a cost albatross that has squeezed the life-giving breath of profit out of many a company.
- The accumulation of unbudgeted expenses will suck the blood out of your business. Unbudgeted expenses mostly come about from spur-of-the-moment decisions. And all of a sudden, expense estimates are hopelessly out of whack. Costs can get out of control not because of some big well-considered commitment but because of a lot of little commitments that are hardly considered at all.

I sometimes find myself feeling sorry for some of our executives who deny themselves the great personal satisfaction of being a manager. Management means being in

84

control. It is the art of preventing surprises, especially unpleasant ones.

In our business, management means being in control of new business and the costs attendant to it, not merely charging off after "opportunities" to pitch. It means planned deployment of personnel, not hiring and firing on the basis of sudden alleged crises. It means knowing what money is coming in and what money is going out, in advance, when the power to create a favorable balance is still in your hands.

Every company has some people who are managers in title only. Strong companies try to keep their number low. Strong managers make strong companies.

The Other Part of the Job

When I was a kid, my father ran a neighborhood grocery store. It was spotless. He had a fetish about quality and freshness—in meat, produce and all the goods that were sold in bulk in those days before frozen foods and convenience packaging. He was a nice man, popular in the neighborhood.

In 1933 his 20-year struggle to build a business came to an end when he sold his shrunken inventory and his bulging accounts receivable for a few cents on the dollar.

He always blamed the chain stores with their lower prices, lower quality, no credit, no delivery, impersonal self-service and heavy advertising of specials. Those policies were an anathema to him.

But he was wrong. In the end, it was not the chain stores but his own sense of values that did him in.

He enjoyed serving his customers and was a very good salesman. He knew their individual likes, he could suggest menus instead of merely filling orders, he was good at suggesting things they hadn't thought about buying—add-ons like olives, relishes, hard candy, snack crackers, things like that.

The trouble was that much of his business was done on credit, and my father was not much interested in what he perceived as a rather embarrassing matter of asking to be paid. It was after their unpaid bills piled up that his customers deserted him for the chains where they spent what cash they had. Even as a child, I was aware that they were skulking out their backdoors and down the alleys to the A&P and National Tea while our family business shriveled up and our suppliers began applying tighter terms.

We are, all of us, products of our heredity and our environment, so perhaps this is why I have such short patience with those of our people who are uninterested in or unwilling to police credit firmly. We have too many people who think their job is done when the billing goes out. Even worse, we have some who seem fearful to bill what the job cost. If a client can't or won't pay promptly for the work he authorizes, we must shed that client quickly, for he is eating our lunch. If we have employees who are unwilling to charge and collect for the work they do, they are redundant to our operation and we should give them a proper push toward the Salvation Army, Red Cross or Mission Society that are legally set up as not-for-profit organizations, which we are not.

Peter Drucker points out that a company can survive for a few years without profit if it has a reasonable cash flow, but not the other way around. Money management is the easiest first step to improved productivity. As Mr. Drucker says, money doesn't charge overtime, takes no sick leave or vacations, requires no retirement fund, works seven days a week and 24 hours a day, and the more intensively you work it the more it will do for you. But to manage it, you must first get it by collecting what is owed you, on time and in full.

Getting the client's job done is only part of getting your job done. The rest is getting paid for it, promptly and in full. Believe me, letting payments slide will only hurt, not help, customer relations. It is not alone a question of whether the client is good for it—even the most affluent tend to become quarrelsome when bills are old, decisions forgotten, people have changed and enthusiasms gone flat. And the less affluent, when the unpaid bills mount, will quit looking you in the eye and start slipping down the alleys to competitors.

Don't adopt the lifestyle of a sucker. If you are proud of what you do, self-respect requires that it be paid for promptly. You have nothing to lose by insisting on regular, businesslike payment except, just possibly, your own inferiority complex.

Fables For Our Times:
Why Leaders Win Price Wars

Deep in the vast and impenetrable forest of southwest Abalonia, there lives a fine featherless species of fowl called the gallakahoochie bird.

Gallakahoochie birds are held in high esteem in the jungle and are often consulted by lions, tigers, elephants, baboons and wildebeests even though, taken as a whole, birds are generally equated with sociology professors. In fact, your run-of-the-woods bird is something of a staple in the Abalonian forest fast-food diet.

But the gallakahoochie bird is of a different stripe. (Actually, light blue on a navy background.) He (or even she, since they practice hen lib) thinks of himself not as a bird but as an important member of the jungle community and a specialist in communications. Sitting on a high branch, he observes what is going on. Or, quietly blending into the tangled thicket, he can hear the cries of animal anguish as the Forest Tail Commission or the Forest Dung Administration (commonly known as the FTC and FDA) institute investigations or hand down restraining orders.

From his objective position, a gallakahoochie bird can advise on what is happening and how the lions and tigers and other jungle leaders can get their roars or bleats listened to. So it came to be that these fine birds developed a confident modesty and learned the value of first getting all the facts and then speaking softly with good humor and conviction and charging a lot of slugs for their services.

But, you ask, why didn't the other birds get in on the action?

Well, the trouble with the crows was that they called attention to themselves, instead of to the lions and tigers, with their impatient "caw, caw, caw" even before they checked wind direction to see which way the sound would carry.

And the magpies, with their incessant chatter, made the elephants nervous but no wiser.

And the parrots kept saying, "Yes, sir!" and repeating what their clients had just said.

The vultures were listened to only in the case of bankruptcy.

Finally a few dodo birds got together and figured out that if they quit researching a problem and put together a couple of all-purpose solutions and dressed like the gallakahoochie in navy with baby blue stripes, they could do the same thing, cut prices and corner the market.

One day some lions were sitting around lapping up juniper berries and branch water and bragging about their favorite consultant gallkahoochie birds.

"I hear there's a new firm of dodo birds in the business," said a mangy king of the jungle. "They claim they have wonderful connections and can do anything the gallakahoochie birds can for much less money. Has anyone tried them?"

"I have," a tough old lion admitted.

The lions all looked at him with interest. "What did you think of them?" they all wanted to know.

"They were delicious," he said.

MORAL: *You can fool all of the cats some of the time and some of the cats all of the time, but, if you fool yourself, you're a barbecued dodo bird.*

Filling the Lily Pond

John Strohm and I were in college together. He went on to become a successful publisher and an authority on conservation, wildlife, and farming. It was he who put together the famous reciprocal visits of Khruschev and a group of American farmers that opened up agricultural trade between the United States and Russia.

John is concerned because we are overfishing our oceans, overcutting our forests, overgrazing our grasslands, and overplowing our soil. To illustrate how rapidly these excesses are catching up with us, he tells of a riddle the French used to teach schoolchildren the nature of exponential growth.

A lily pond, so the riddle goes, contains a single leaf. Each day the number of leaves in the pond doubles—two leaves the second day, four on the third, eight on the fourth, and so on. If the lily pond is completely full on the thirtieth day, the riddle asks, when is it half full? The answer is: on the twenty-ninth day.

This simple lesson explains many things that affect our lives; some are good, some are dangerous or even disastrous. John Strohm sees the growth of the world's population combined with the depletion of resources proceeding at a rate that will suddenly consume civilization if drastic curbs are not imposed far ahead of the thirtieth day.

The principle, however, can be put to great advantage. For instance, it took us many years of steady growth at the rate of about 15 percent a year to get big enough to be noticed. We doubled every five years but on a small base so the results weren't dramatic. It took us about the same time to grow from a $1,000,000 business to a $2,000,000 business as it did to grow from $150,000,000 to $300,000,000.

The principle has much to do with how some people have become wealthy without striking oil, inheriting an estate, or finding buried treasures. I am well acquainted with a number of people who have had the character to live within their income, however modest it might be at any given time, and put aside a bit of it year after year in conservative investments to let compounding interest work its magic. What seems so slow at first ultimately becomes a fantastic gain as time goes on, though the numerical rate is unchanged.

Several years ago I was present at an IBM meeting when Thomas Watson, then the chairman, was challenged on his goal of continued growth of at least 15 percent annually, to double every five years, just as this has been our goal. A security analyst said that this would ultimately make IBM bigger than the gross national product and was therefore an unattainable long-range objective.

Mr. Watson said, approximately: "Perhaps, but we've done it up to now and we expect to do it next year. We'll just have to keep trying."

I feel very much the same way. I don't know what we can't do; I do know what we have done.

Even when things seem to move more slowly than I would like, even when we fall a bit behind our plan for new business, or new kinds of business, or profits or whatever, I keep my faith in the principle of compounding, comforted by my absolute belief that if we keep plugging away making some progress, time is always on our side.

Little Boxes

In a new business presentation the other day, a prospective client asked for a copy of our organization chart. I explained we didn't have one, but if he was into that sort of thing, we'd make one up for him.

You see, we do know how to draw those little boxes and connect them with solid and dotted lines in pyramidal progression. In fact we used to do that from time to time. I even went to a swell do at the National Industrial Conference Board for two days to learn about different evasive titles and functions with which to label the little boxes.

Organization charts may be peachy at General Electric, Mannesmann Steel, or the Department of Health, Education and Welfare where at the very least they will serve the same purpose as laundry marks. But in a business like ours—or at least a company like ours—they usually generate some heat but no light.

No two of our offices run quite the same way, despite the fact that they operate under the same code of ethics and with the same operating principles. And that's just fine.

What makes a company fly or flop is people, not functions, not titles, not organization charts. And people are different. Two general managers can be equally successful and run their jobs and deploy their corps de ballet in wholly different patterns. Two account executives can be on a par in productivity, profit, creativity, and get similar results in quite dissimilar ways.

For people to be happy and to accomplish the most, they must have some freedom to capitalize on their strengths and to shape their job in the same general outline that shapes their own pluses and minuses. It is not inconsistent to ask that everyone in a given business (on a given team, citizens of a given country—whatever) obey a common set of rules or laws enacted for the general welfare. That doesn't prevent establishing a climate where people are respected as individuals and recognized as unique.

Organization charts, for whatever else they may do, tend to force these unique people into single job mechanisms and ultimately the opportunity to be far better than average is edited out. On top of that, organization charts proliferate organization. Empty boxes must be filled.

I could write more on this subject but I have to leave to attend a meeting of the board of trustees of the American Management Associations. Please don't turn me in for being a fink.

The Increment of Staying in Business

Damn, how it used to cob me to pick up the trade press and read that some account ideally suited to us had changed agencies and we hadn't even been invited in for a sniff.

It still happens, of course, but not often in those locations where we've been around long enough to put down deep and wide-spreading roots.

In those places, simply by being there and visible long enough, we are the beneficiaries of the increment of staying in business.

When we were young, impatient and often frustrated, a very wise observer of business explained to me the increment of staying in business.

"In all business, but particularly service business," he said, "a company can start with excellent people and a good idea and yet, in spite of everything, disappointments will outnumber triumphs five to one. People are just more comfortable giving their trade to somebody who's been in business a while and whose success and stability are evident.

"Then, later on, a company can actually be slipping badly, with good people retired and work mediocre, and still attract new clients, who may be intrigued with the eager, high-visibility new companies but wind up rationalizing themselves into the stables of the old."

The trick, of course, is to keep the faith early on. Then to keep up the momentum, the enthusiasm, the ideals which gave the company the courage to start up. And finally, to adopt corporate self-renewal as a way of life.

The Suggestion Box

I have often been asked—twice, I think it was—why we do not have employee suggestion boxes on our premises. OK, I'll tell you.

During World War II or the Boer War (I forget which), I

was advertising manager at a manufacturing plant. As our only customer was the U.S. government, there was no one to whom to advertise so I was given divers other duties. Among them, I was put in charge of employee jollies and morale.

That included attending ethnic weddings, running the plant golf and bowling leagues, planning the annual picnic, distracting government expediters with Northern Indiana hooch, and operating the company suggestion system. This explains why I have such low regard for the Polish hop, bowling, large families, potato salad and locally refined grain neutral spirits. Also suggestion boxes.

You would never believe what people put in suggestion boxes. For instance, chewing gum wrappers. I cite gum wrappers because they are one of the good things. Most suggestion box deposits cannot be mentioned in a semi-public journal such as this without risk of a worldwide loss of lunch or at least grievous offense to human dignity.

Of course, along with imaginative garbage you do get a few suggestions. The most common one is a variously worded recommendation that the management commit self-immolation. A subclassification in the anonymous or nom-de-plume category is the gossip epistle through which management learns that Tessie is raunching around with Albert whose wife thinks he spends his evenings at the YMCA lifting weights. Or that Herman in accounting sleeps at his desk.

Now and then under three used sweat socks and a bookmark inscribed "Prepare to Meet Thy God," there is a genuine suggestion intended to increase sales, lower costs, improve service, add to the line, or some such laudable objective. Unfortunately, regardless of what you may have read elsewhere, the useful yield is very low.

A high percentage will involve the expenditure of considerable capital sums, such as for buying out all larger competitors or piping in recorded country music. A few will propose setting up departments to specialize in new trends like horticulture. Or, "Let's revive the company picnic and see how Tessie and Albert behave with all their kids around."

Now all of this probably sounds as if we're closed minded, smug and omnipotent. I swear to you, very much the opposite. It's just that experience teaches that good people with good ideas can't wait to talk about them and come running to get them considered.

In a business like ours, where creation is constant and indeed is what our business is about, a formalized suggestion system seems to inhibit rather than promote ideation. Putting up boxes seems only to encourage the sadly insecure snarks who want to be heard but are afraid to be seen. The really sincere people with a hot idea will have no inhibitions about getting the message to Garcia.

(Signed)
Garcia

Hot Shops

A few weeks ago, the *New York Times* called us a "hot shop." Some of my associates thought that was simply delightful. It did a little less for me.

I am not very hypertensive about this "hot" label for agencies. It is usually applied for the wrong reasons and all too often attaches itself to the loosely carpentered agency of some ego-driven smart-ass who has repainted some old ideas with a new synthetic covering.

At the moment, in the United States we are seeing the public embarrassment of a public relations firm that from this distance seems to have let opportunism lead policy. This was the "hot shop" of a few years ago.

We have seen the drowning during the last couple of years of several advertising agencies whose principals were often quoted while apparently walking on water.

My definition of a "hot shop" is a little different than that of the trade press columnists.

I think a hot shop is one that grows and prospers, year after year.

One which recruits, trains, keeps and promotes good people.

One that really cares about the quality and economic usefulness of its work.

One that has a code of business ethics and lives by it.

That summary very well defines several advertising and public relations agencies. They are the ones that get and keep good clients, often without undue tambourine banging on street corners.

Fables for Our Times: Old Friends Are the Best Friends

Once upon a time there was a client that had had the same agency for many years. The client people and the agency people had gotten very used to each other. You might say they took each other for granted.

The agency knew that last year's program was well received, so it kept putting out more of the same. The client kept approving more of the same because business was pretty good and, anyway, it was sort of nice not to have to make new decisions or take chances on something different.

There came a day when the client got a new director of market research and, having nothing else to do, he did some research. It showed the client was losing market share. Being new and brash, he mentioned his findings to the president, who found this very interesting, especially since one of his directors, whose wife was a sister of nine agency presidents, mentioned that her brothers thought the company's advertising and public relations were both dated.

So the president called in the agency and said, "You know, we've been together a long time and perhaps we should be taking a new look at what other sources are available."

And the agency said, "Oh, sir, let us bring you up to date first on all the wonderful things we are capable of doing nowadays, and let us show you some super great fantastic exciting original orgiastic ideas for your wonderful company."

"Fine," said the client. "We are certainly going to give you every chance. We have invited nine other agencies to make a presentation to us, and you, our old and devoted friends, shall be the tenth. And we wish you the best of luck."

MORAL: *A pitch in time saves nine.*

The Glamourous Pursuit of Sardines

Just about everyone in advertising or public relations loves new business.

When a chance to compete for a big new account comes along, people go ape. Slow movers run, early quitters work all night, old hands quiver, trainees go into a trance, and adolescent pustules break out on senior management.

And in between these Presentations Grande, in agencies all over the world, new business committees pick over the bones of identical target prospect lists and fantasize strategic plans for ingratiating themselves with inaccessible and disinterested client executives.

From the slightly cynical tone of this you may conclude that I don't care much for the pursuit of new business. Not so at all. I love it. I think it is the second most important part of our business. But it is second.

The most important thing (and by a wide margin) is *old* business—keeping and developing the accounts we already have.

A lot of so-called "hot" shops with splashy new business records have gone belly-up because they couldn't hang on to the clients they got with fancy footwork and peachy promises. It costs heavy gelt to keep new business activity at a compulsive level, and if the clients come and go in a short period, the relationship between costs and income can be ruinous.

If we want to be a great agency, we must glamorize old business. We must put the same imagination, enthusiasm and dedication against the communications programs of those companies who have already chosen us as those we are merely wooing. We must give at least as much recognition to those of our people who develop strong, mutually productive relationships with old clients as we do to those who help bring in new ones.

Sometimes when I see us lusting after a spavined, swaybacked prospect, I have to wonder what the same amount of crash creativity applied to one of our solid, credit-worthy corporate leader clients would accomplish. It would certainly be more profitable.

The way agencies get so mesmerized by new business reminds me of the old sardine story.

There's this canner who has a huge inventory of not entirely fresh sardines. He calls his jobber and says, "I got some special labeled sardines—10,00 gross. You're a good guy; I'll make you a deal—50 percent off." The jobber couldn't possibly get rid of that many, but the deal was too good to pass up. He took the lot, sold some of it to his wholesalers and traded the rest to another jobber for 6,000 gross of canned tomatoes. That jobber sold some of the sardines to his wholesalers and traded the rest to another jobber for 3,000 gross of canned peas. That jobber sold some sardines and traded the rest to another jobber for 1,000 gross of canned beans. The last jobber got rid of all but 1,000 cases of sardines and called the first jobber who was long on tomatoes, so he took back 500 cases of sardines in exchange and called another jobber who was long on peas and traded off all but 50 cases for peas. He was having a party so he took a case of sardines home. His wife opened can after can, and they were all spoiled.

Next day he called the canner. "Those sardines you sold me were spoiled. I couldn't eat them."

"Of course not," the canner said. "Those sardines

were 50 percent off. They weren't for eating; they were for trading."

And sometimes I wonder if new business is more for the chase than the embrace.

Fables for Our Times: How to Avoid Insomnia

The way to make the most money in most businesses is to have a very few large clients or customers instead of a large number of smaller ones.

It is a more precarious way to live, however. When our agency was adolescent, nearly 80 percent of our income came from two clients—Rockwell and Clark.

Colonel Rockwell had four daughters and one son, and George Spatta, his counterpart at Clark, had four sons and a daughter. I used to have these nightmares where, in a double wedding, a couple of the Colonel's kids married a couple of Spatta's and started an advertising agency. I woke up sweating.

I had a friend who manufactured paint. He had only five big customers for private brands. In one year, two of them got a new source of supply and my friend went from a $210,000 profit one year to a $350,000 loss the next.

In my time, I've known a dozen agencies that spilled their guts all over the sidewalk when the basket in which they had all their eggs came unwoven.

An agency I know has 70 percent of its considerable volume with one client. If the client president sneezes while hunting aardvark in Africa, the agency president instinctively holds out a tissue in New York.

That's the way to maximize profit but minimize sleep. Which of these is more important is a matter of corporate philosophy. Our choice has been to make a little less and relax a little more.

MORAL: *Better beans and bacon in peace than cakes and ale in fear.*

What Consultants Can't Do

Having been both a buyer and a seller of consulting services, I think I know why most definitions of a consultant are either cynical or weak attempts at humor.

When I put on my sincere tie and my pin stripe consultant's suit, I try for humility by reciting one such definition:

> A consultant is a person who knows
> nothing about your business to whom
> you pay more to tell you how to run it
> than you could earn if you ran it right
> instead of the way he tells you.

A consultant, like a physician, can diagnose and prescribe, but if you want to get well, you have to take the medicine yourself. So often a consultant disappoints because after he helps you define the problem and probably suggests a plan to attack it, he stops, lacking the authority, responsibility and acceptance to put it into effect.

The hard truth is that you can buy advice, sympathy and understanding for management problems just as easily as for sexual problems, but in either case the successful orgasm depends upon your own performance.

Auld Lang Syne

The other day Wally Vartan came to see me in Chicago. Wally is a remarkable guy. He knows half of Chicago. He was a buddy of Mayor Daley. When Wally's daughter was married, she left the reception in the fire commissioner's red Cadillac with sirens wailing.

But Wally is much more than that. He is one of a group of people who have helped build our company almost as much as any employee. He has been an absolutely dedicated, honest and dependable supplier since the days we opened our doors. He and his sons run Lake Shore Photoengraving. When they were little, we were little, and we grew together. And we stayed together.

Wally dropped in to say thanks for our growing volume of business, but especially for sticking with him through a difficult strike. It was the least we could do for a guy like Wally.

This memo could have just as easily started with Jim Chalifoux or Harvey Peate or Eddie Steward, God rest his soul. They are all suppliers and friends and supporters and have been right from the start.

We have a conscious policy of sticking with our vendors. It has paid off in a thousand ways. We get service and quality and cooperation that others are unable to buy. We deal with these old friends in complete candor. If we have a problem, it's also theirs and hopefully it works both ways. We deal directly with owners and managers and, believe me, that means preferential treatment in every way.

In nearly every case, we are one of the biggest accounts in the house. And it's all been done without fancy presents or kickbacks which are—or at least used to be—quite common in the graphic arts business. All we want is a good price, superb quality and miraculous service.

Staying with suppliers extends over to our professional counselors, too. We've had the same public accounting firm all 28 years, the same law firm for 27-plus years. We jiggled around a little more with banks because a couple didn't take us seriously. Mel Anshen has been a consultant for something like 24 years.

When things go wrong with one of these suppliers or advisers—and sometimes they have—it's easy to get it cleared up. We know and trust each other. We've dropped suppliers only when, after laying our problems on the table, nothing happened.

Sometimes I wonder about those companies that you read are always changing advertising or public relations agencies. They must be awfully insecure. The advantages of staying with dedicated people whose future depends upon yours seem so self-evident and self-satisfying that they are missing so much.

Loyalty is not purchasable. It is also not unilateral. It grows and thrives on mutual understanding and respect. To be gotten, it must be given.

Who Owns This Joint?

Every now and then someone says something that makes me realize that, in spite of our promiscuous practice of shareholder democracy, there are lingering suspicions that I own all, or nearly all, of the company. Don't I wish!

It's true that I was beside the manger at the delivery. It is also true that my name, frequently misspelled, identifies our enterprise, but that is at least partly because I outlived the other original principal stockholders.

Today, like 113 others of you, I am a minority shareholder. Of course, my minority is better than anyone else's minority, but it is shrinking, and any time a reasonable number of the other owners become adequately impatient they could throw me out on my butt. It makes a person think twice about whom one insults.

It was not always thus. To get this venture off the ground, E. A. Gebhardt contributed the net worth of his agency, Gebhardt & Brockson. It was $90,000. Rod Reed contributed the net worth of the McCarty Company of Pennsylvania and also some cash, adding up to $45,000. I used savings, borrowings and some sales of other stocks I had accumulated to put $90,000 into our original capitalization and we three took stock in those proportions.

From the start we made it possible for other employees to acquire stock at book value, exactly as we had done. Meanwhile, prior to retirement, Gebhardt started selling stock to the company for ultimate reissue to other employees and to me. To raise the further capital we needed to finance growth, we also issued some additional stock, mostly to me which I again financed by borrowing. It was quite a while before the stock belonged to me instead of the banks and I could sleep normally again.

When Rod Reed died we were in good enough shape for the company to reacquire his stock and make it available to employees.

Meanwhile I started a plan of gradual reduction of stock holdings so that in the event I died suddenly, the company or its principal shareholders would not face a financial crisis. Through some sales and some gifts to charitable foundations who resold to our employees, my relative share of ownership has been steadily reduced. Of course, as stock was issued for acquisitions, that had some of the same effect. Since our stock has a way of doubling in value every five years or so, I have prospered as has everyone else who, like me, made a financial commitment years ago.

It has turned out to be my best investment by far. That has also been true of a great many others, including some loyal and courageous people who through self-denial found the funds to acquire small amounts of stock when they became eligible. I have a special feeling about them. We believed in each other and, what do you know, it turned out all right.

Political Accounts*

During this political season, I have been asked several times why we don't handle political accounts.

It certainly isn't because we haven't been asked. In the last four or five years, we have shied away from a variety of requests in several offices and from both parties.

As a matter of policy, we have concluded that most political candidates don't represent the kind of clients for whom we wish to work. There are some good reasons.

---

*From "The Wonderful World of Words"

In the first place, handling a political campaign is highly disruptive to the regular conduct of business. For a relatively short period of time, it demands excessive attention, puts people under great pressure, and undoubtedly shortchanges regular clients who pay our bills year in and year out.

Second, we are uneasy about putting our employees in the position of working on a political account when their ideology may be totally opposed to that of the candidate. This applies not only to the account and creative staff but to service department personnel as well, who not infrequently in a political campaign are expected to work all night or right through several consecutive weekends, often for somebody they abhor.

Third, the history of agency-political relations is studded with financial difficulties. As emotions rise and panic sets in toward the end of a campaign, caution and budgets go out the window and many an agency has found itself eating the final costs of a campaign with no recourse against a candidate, his party, or more likely, a spurious committee that goes out of business the minute the polls close.

Finally, and most important of all, political advertising is very often dirty advertising. An awful lot of what I have heard and seen during the recent political campaign is far below the ethical standards of this agency.

It is especially galling to me to see some of the political advertising for candidates who have been so critical of commercial advertising, often attacking it as untruthful or at best misleading and distorted. These same politicians, working on their own behalf, employ people whose business morals are well below those of most good agencies and then encourage them to produce advertising that, if it were for a corporation or for a product, would be in trouble with the FTC, the FCC, the FDA, the Department of Justice, and a half dozen other assorted agencies and commissions.

It seems to me that it might not be a bad idea to play back some of the campaign tapes during the assorted witch-hunting investigations of advertising.

Understanding People; Anyway, Some People

When something goes wrong, the first place most of us look is somewhere else. Even when the evidence unmistakably points our way, human nature is such that we seem conditioned to, at the very least, find a co-conspirator.

Our natural reaction is like the woman who said to her husband, "Dear, don't you think you ought not to drink any more? Your face is getting fuzzy."

Creative Management

Senility has no direct relationship to a specific age; it comes first and most virulently, however, to egotists and board chairmen. There is no warning, as in the case of heart trouble, through shortness of breath. Rather it is likely to be characterized by longness of breath and an increasing infatuation with the past. Unfortunately, the past tends to be dated and dull.

* * * *

Beware of Association Junkies, the people who spend half their time going to association meetings, conferences, briefings, conventions and miscellaneous gatherings of the clan. Between times they can drop names, relay their misinterpretation of what some thought-leader said and choose from their surfeit of trivia in such a manner as to keep the subject at hand away from everyday problem solving. They are often pleasant, well-mannered and moderately interesting people. They are also expert on the rooms to avoid at the Waldorf, Drake, Fairmont, Century Plaza and Shamrock-Hilton. They know the best menu choices at the Greenbrier, Homestead, Breakers and Broadmoor.

The trouble is, they toil not, neither do they spin.

* * * *

I want no communion with doomsayers. Optimists are much better companions and far more likely to breed success.

* * * *

Uncle Fred could always find something good to say about everyone. For instance, when he was challenged to find something nice to say about a notoriously mean, cheap, antisocial neighbor, he said, "Well, he doesn't let his dog go on the sidewalk." He had a theory that most people's bad traits were just overcompensation for some terrible unseen burden so he was so full of compassion it almost gave you diabetes.

But he sure did have a lot of friends, some of them you wouldn't want. When he died he had the best attended funeral of the year, and some people said he looked wonderful, though of course he couldn't hear them.

Eight months later Aunt Bertha married the Superintendent of the State Reform School. Well, whatever turns you on. Or off, for that matter.

In Search of Status

Different people see status quite differently.

In the work world, the same symbols that some people pant over are looked upon as somewhere between unimportant and puerile by others.

I have seen people on their hands and knees measuring their newly assigned offices to be sure they weren't any smaller than one assigned to someone else in the same job category.

I have solemnly considered propositions to create exotic and meaningless titles for otherwise rational people who somehow needed an external sign of reassurance that they were appreciated. Management consultants who specialize in employee compensation will tell you that for some people a high title is more urgent and a greater reward than a high salary.

On the other hand, some publicly held companies, where top executive salaries must be disclosed, have found that there are people—contrary to what most of us would believe—who welcome the publicity as a sign of success.

Some rich and aging people like to be seen with the young and glamorous of the opposite sex as evidence that they are still virile and attractive. Of course, there may be other reasons, too, but never mind.

Anyway, the pursuit of status symbols ranks with the common cold as one of man's most persistent minor maladies. In place of bed rest, aspirin and fruit juice, the indicated antidote for ordinary status seeking is a sense of humor. People who can laugh at themselves rarely develop the serious complications of consumptive self-adoration and high-temperature jealousy.

Actually, the only real status comes from one's own ability and from a sensitivity to others. There is no true status in a corner office. Windows on two sides merely let in more light so that competence or incompetence can be more quickly detected.

The people in this world who are admired are the ones who are perceived to be able, dedicated and helpful to others. Trappings and titles have very little to do with lasting judgments of true status; in fact, it seems they are as often an impediment as they are a help in gaining the respect of those around us. The reward of great generals is not a bigger tent but the pride of accomplishment and the affection of the troops.

In every organization, people know full well who has status and who doesn't and a chart on the wall may have little to do with the real assignment of power.

Status is earned, not granted, and then must be earned again and again as times and the players change. As we get older and more perceptive from years of sorting out the real ones from the phonies, the external symbols mean less and less.

Although I must say I still like to see my name on the door. I just try not to genuflect as I push it open.

On Being What You Are

During World War II, I worked at a manufacturing plant in East Chicago, Indiana. For those of you with fuzzy familiarity with the geography of the U.S. midlands, if you did a rectal examination of the Greater Chicago area, you'd come across East Chicago right away.

It is an area of tight little enclaves of first and second generation immigrants with roots in at least a dozen European countries. One of my duties was representing management at ethnic weddings. It was very important to their tribal status that some ranking "boss" turn up at these nuptial assemblages. That's how I got to be a vice president of my company, so that no legitimate vice president would have to learn to polka.

Living and working among these people taught me a lot, but the lesson that has been the most useful is not to try to be something you are not.

To them I was a "boss," and got acceptance, respect and friendship in direct relation to how I performed as a boss. If I tried too hard to be one of them, communication ended. If a Lithuanian wanted camaraderie, he got it at the neighborhood bar; if he had personal problems, he took them to the parish priest—unless the priest happened to be Irish, German or Italian, in which case he took them to the president of the Lithuanian Savings and Loan.

A lot of advertisements and a lot of public relations programs fail because the creator has tried to be something he is not. It is said that a good writer can write about anything. Perhaps, but often without conviction.

On the other hand, a good reporter can usually report fairly accurately on the findings, experiences, beliefs or aspirations of others. It is not necessary to have a degree in mechanical engineering to write a good case history on a steam-generating plant as long as you listen carefully, report correctly and write enthusiastically. Then ask a qualified engineer to check your accuracy.

In technical writing, the procedure seems obvious. In writing about everyday products and situations, there is a great temptation to assume you know more than you do, are more typical than you are, and understand things that only personal experience can teach.

Shirley Polykoff wrote great ads for Clairol partly because she had been coloring her hair for years. She knew the motivations firsthand. David Ogilvy wrote beautifully about Rolls-Royce. He lived a Rolls-Royce life.

We are what we are. Trying to be otherwise almost always shows up in a subtle absence of believability.

Our Secret Burdens

I have never met anyone so poised, so glamorous, so successful, so healthy, so blithe, so rich, so calm, so personable, so self-sufficient, so spaced out, so anything that underneath they didn't have some considerable limitations. And if they don't have problems now, if they live long enough, they will acquire them before they depart this earth.

You, as I, have probably known easy-going people whose guts have suddenly erupted with ulcers. Or the perfect marriage that ended with a dramatically imperfect divorce. The business, political, professional or theological success who is deposed. The rich man whose loans are called. The glamorous woman who one day sees in a mirror a middle-aged stranger whose beauty is spent.

Who knows how many self-sufficient people cry out in the night from loneliness? How many seemingly happy people are really possessed by anxiety?

It is human nature to construct a facade that hides imperfections, doubts, fears, worries, and inner conflict. Thank God. Think how miserable we could make each other if we continuously let it all hang out.

However, it is because we really know so little about what goes on inside of others that envy exists. If you can learn to accept as gospel the fact that everyone has or will develop secret burdens, you have acquired the antidote for the very human trait of jealousy.

When I read that the head of some business is making $500,000 a year, I think, "Poor bastard, think of his tax problems!" When I read some gorgeous woman has said, "I am so happy—I have an understanding husband, a great lover and fine children," I believe that she is at the center of a turbulent sea of unhappiness in which she will ultimately drown. And when I read about the dropouts who have renounced worldly goods and organized society to live in communal love, I thank goodness I don't have to exist among the dirty dishes and shared b.o.

A business, like any other organizational entity of our culture, succeeds to the extent it encourages its members to interchange their strengths and subdue their weaknesses. As John F. Kennedy (and many others) said, "Life is not easy." If a good looking, rich, charismatic, powerful, articulate leader like him had inner turmoil and frequent unhappiness, who are we to be envious of anyone?

Overrating

It's probably a natural tendency, but most of us have a contagious habit of overrating employees on performance evaluations, salary increase requests, etc.

Also, some of us get carried away by our warm feelings for our associates and feel compelled to dash off letters full of rhetoric ordinarily associated with the Nobel Prize or the Congressional Medal of Honor.

For the most part, in the past these exaggerated ratings and encomiums have been harmless fur-stroking. But the world, she is a-changing.

In many countries, there are new regulations proposed or already in effect that provide for employees' access to their personnel files and, in the event they were terminated, may put the burden of proof on the employer as to whether or not the sacking was justified.

Many times I've read evaluations that, if they were to be believed, would lead to the inevitable conclusion that indeed we should reverse the positions of the manager and the managee since, so far as I can observe, there are no managers who are excellent in absolutely everything. Yet I can cite case after case of terminating someone only months after he or she was elevated to sainthood on a performance or salary review form or via a gushy letter commemorating the successful completion of a routine assignment.

This is investing in future problems. Be realistic. Only very, very few people are truly excellent in any category, and most of us are merely adequate in most. That doesn't mean someone can't be considered for a raise or a promotion.

Overinflated evaluations will sooner or later eat your lunch. If you want to praise someone, use the telephone or, better yet, person to person. The letter you write may well turn up in strange and embarrassing places.

After all, we are mere mortals, all of us. Even the people who work for you.

Another Hard-Won Triumph

When we get a new account, memos fly around the world heaping praise on presenters, researchers, artists, writers, slide makers, preparers of coffee and tea, the goodness of the human race in general and the greatness of our brand of humankind in particular.

But when we lose an account, it is as if a conspiracy of silence pulls a black cloth over the corpus delicti of what was once described as an account of extraordinary magnificence and health, until the trade press takes note of the change and it is no longer possible to hide the fact that we must have done something wrong.

I always wonder how those wonderful people, listed with such care in the first memo for their role in the Conquest of Rome, are never identified when what they bring us is Pearl Harbor.

Perhaps it is just that we have so many samples of new business success memos that it is easy to find a pattern to follow for any occasion. Perhaps it is only because we have no guide for memos covering the old heave-ho that none ever appears. Therefore, I have crafted one which, with minor tinkering, should cover many forms of demise. To wit:

> TO: All Personnel, Their Families and Creditors
> FROM: Your Current General Manager
> SUBJECT: Intercontinental Products, Inc., Ltd.

> Today we received a terse letter from Raymond P. Thompson-Bates, Communications Vice President of Intercontinental Products, informing us of their decision to hire a new advertising and public relations agency. Our disengagement is effective day before yesterday.

> This is no ordinary account we are losing. Intercontinental is not only the world leader in clotheslines and musk oil but their management is famous for tolerance, fairness and abhorrence of unpleasant decisions. To have been sacked is a

testimony to what we can accomplish if we all pull together.

Special recognition should go to a lot of people. On the advertising side, Mr. Thompson-Bates especially singled out Ron Le Fleur, who quit writing conference reports a year ago; Helen Hunker, who sent the musk oil ad to *Laundry & Detergent News;* and Pat Martinovich of Accounting, who made life easier by sending Intercontinental someone else's billing for six consecutive months. He also had special words for Eunice Halestrom and Herschel Flipside for their ability to recreate the Central Park Lagoon in the Samoan Islands for the "Hemp is Better" clothesline commercial for only $331,962.07.

Mr. Thompson-Bates wanted you to know he was not motivated by our advertising people alone. He commented particularly that he would have mentioned our public relations account executives by name if any had been on the account for more than 60 days. He did recall Richard Yale, however, as the one who called to say he wouldn't be around Intercontinental any longer since he had been promoted to a larger and more profitable account.

He also mentioned how impressed he was with the sales promotion department and the job they did on the new catalog. With only seven months' notice, they got started on it the Friday afternoon before the Hawaii convention and by getting suppliers to work all weekend at only double time, we delivered 500 catalogs to Hawaii only three days after the convention ended. Despite the incredible pressure, the job was done with only two minor typographical errors—the client's name was misspelled on the cover and Page six was set in Chinese.

Mr Thompson-Bates has offered to tell any prospective client who asks all about us. It is really working together like this that we can foul up an account. On behalf of all of us in management who did our part by staying strictly away from Intercontinental for more than two years, I want to thank you all, especially those of you who will soon be leaving.

(signed)
Your Current General Manager

People I Don't Understand*

I don't understand people who never look out the window on a plane and who never use the map in the seat pocket.

I don't understand people who, in a strange city, want to be driven instead of renting a car and finding their own way.

Or people who can go to a supermarket and buy only the things they came for.

I don't understand people without a sense of loyalty or people who find disenchantment chic.

Or people who avoid talking to taxi drivers.

Or habitual cynics who are quick to criticize and add nothing of value.

I don't understand people who aren't upset if they miss an easy putt.

I don't understand closed minded people who call themselves liberals.

I understand why some people are stuffy, but I don't understand how stuffy people can be oblivious to their own stuffiness.

I don't understand dumb Kansans who won't listen to smart New Yorkers. Or dumb New Yorkers who sneer at smart Kansans.

---

*From "The Wonderful World of Words."

I don't understand people who can live in Rome without bothering to learn Italian.

I don't understand people who are proud of their low threshold of ambition.

I don't understand people who, able to run, only walk slowly.

I don't understand people who listen only for dissonance and cacophony and sniff after that which is putrid.

Or those people who are sighted but, with so much to see and absorb, choose partial blindness as a way of life.

I don't understand those who find it so hard to say, "I love you."

And therefore, I don't understand those people who spend a lifetime in business without discovering the elements of achievement and happiness.

People I Can Very Nicely Do Without*

- People who delegate trivia but never delegate responsibility.
- Office politicians.
- People who don't answer a ringing phone unless it's theirs.
- People who suck lemons in front of piccolo players.
- People who think the customer's business is a bore.
- Girls who never dress like girls.
- People who go around putting the knock on their own company but haven't the courage to quit.
- People who don't treat secretaries as equals.
- Secretaries who think they're doing us a favor to come to work.
- People who push suppliers around.

---

*From "The Wonderful World of Words."

Creative Management

- Big Shots who are too important to learn our basic systems and procedures.
- People who never pass the salt unless they're asked.
- People who can't keep a confidence.
- People with dirty fingernails.
- People who call conferences and leave the conference room a mess afterward.
- Writers who resist editing.
- College students who send 25-page questionnaires expecting me to write their dumb theses.
- People who let their dogs lick you.
- People who, like me, never listen.
- All people who are self-important, self-centered and insensitive to others.

Advice to the Young and Such of the Old Who May Never Learn

I believe every cat, regardless of his job, should keep a clean sandbox.

Creative Management

The three rules of the British Foreign Office are very useful to a manager:

- Never tell a lie.
- Never betray a confidence.
- Never pass up a chance to go to the toilet.

* * * *

The beatification of the past can develop the kind of self-satisfaction that fuzzes over the greater wonder, the greater opportunity, the greater joy of the future. Progress doesn't just happen; it is made to happen. And when it does, it brings with it a driving sense of immediacy, and it takes a merciless toll on the inept and undermotivated.

* * * *

I believe that anyone who makes a speech that takes more than 30 minutes is an egotist or a bore. Frequently both.

* * * *

I believe that bigots come in all shapes and colors, from New York as well as Mississippi, are found as frequently among the old as the young, and that there are just as many on the left as the right.

* * * *

When I graduated from college I applied for an opening as Assistant Publicity Manager of the Merchandise Mart in Chicago. It was the best job around that year and it finally got down to a classmate and me. I was sure I would be picked—I thought my qualifications were clearly better—but they took him. I went back to find out why and the personnel manager told me I looked too young to inspire confidence in the older tenants with whom I'd have to deal, so they hired the other guy who was almost bald at 22.

But I got even. I hung on to my hair and the last time I saw him he looked like a chipped cue ball.

Looking young is one disease that sooner or later runs its course. You can count on it.

* * * *

Only the socially secure should order a peanut butter and jelly sandwich for lunch.

118

Some Things I Know For Sure

Fifty percent of advertising copywriters are descended from parrots, 35 percent are descended from speechless peacocks, and the rest are descended straight from God.

Good account executives are very careful about detail, even though it bores them.

You can't administer successful employee relations programs for Midland, Texas, from New York City.

In general, American WASP cooking is very bad, as is Irish cooking. This explains Boston.

New business presentations are like the *Racing Form.* Most of the necessary information is there, but hunch and emotion still color most bets. Then, too, you never know when the fix is in.

Young people should eat lots of chocolate cake because they'll miss it so much when they get older.

There is a correlation between how much Walter Mitty you have in you and how creative you are.

People with a lot of ideas but not much ability at follow-through can get a company into a lot of trouble.

Arrogance is the antithesis of real communication.

Dull people always write dull copy, but bright people write bright copy only when they work hard at it.

Many things contribute to a successful advertisement, but the most important single element is an unmistakable indentification of the product or the sponsor company.

The best way to improve your writing is to write. Every day. Including Christmas, Yom Kippur and the Fourth of July.

Every good creative person I ever met had a wide streak of self-doubt.

Client sales management can't resist a really good selling or merchandising idea even if the budget is already spent. Yet they can sometimes resist a solid advertising idea even if there is still money in the budget.

You can make a good PR man into a good advertising man (or vice versa) easier than you can make a mediocre PR man into a good PR man or a mediocre advertising man into a good advertising man.

I am very nervous about the self-impressed hotshots who think they can wing it at a presentation. Even Laurence Olivier is better if he rehearses.

Most secretaries are more competent than their bosses take the trouble to discover.

From sending out and receiving hundreds of reference letters, as well as phone calls, I've come to two firm conclusions: (a) most people fib a little to a new employer about what they made on the job they are leaving; (b) most people fib a little to their friends at the old job about what they're getting at the new one.

There is no difference between men and women in the qualities that make good account executives or writers. Which is not to decry the difference between men and women.

Some people think visually, some people think verbally and some people don't think much at all. I see no advantage between the first two types.

Maintaining a neat desk and office creates less pressure than working under messy conditions. I used to work in a newspaper office and in a manufacturing plant; I've tried it both ways.

New Yorkers generally know a lot about sociology and very little about geography.

Fish is better on the East Coast, salads are better on the West Coast, and steak and corn on the cob are best in the Midwest. Turnips are the same everywhere.

Don't Take My Advice

One of the hardest things for a manager to learn is not to give certain kinds of advice, even when asked. There is a big difference between being a supervisor and an oracle.

As a matter of strict policy, we tell managers absolutely not to hand out opinions in the "Three M's"—Money, Matrimony, and Medicine. Since there are trained professionals who don't know what they are talking about in at least two of these three areas either, untrained amateurs can get themselves into very deep water very quickly.

Most people have sense enough to leave doctoring to licensed practitioners, but I marvel at how many busybodies, freqently themselves in hock to Beneficial Finance and with a romantic score of two on a scale of ten, are perfectly willing to pass out pearls of investment wisdom or to unravel someone else's misalliance.

So, if you are a boss, keep your lack of genius in the occult arts of health, wealth and stealth to yourself. And if you are among the bossed, take your problems to your neighborhood banker, lawyer, priest, gynecologist, shrink or bartender. Among them you'll find someone fully as incompetent in these matters as the person you work for.

How to Succeed in Business When Really Trying

When I retired, I fully expected to be interviewed by some pubescent tradepaper stringer who would want to know what advice I had for the young on how to achieve success in advertising or public relations.

But if I wait until someone asks me, a whole generation of eager young men and women will have been deprived of this priceless advice and therefore presumably will have failed. So leave us have at it now, in the greening of spring, when there are so many fresh, young, post-academic souls to be saved.

- Lacking prosperous parents or a rich spouse, you will be forced to work quite hard even if you are blessed with uncommon talent.
- Lacking, at one and the same time, uncommon talent, a willingness to work long hours, a rich spouse or loaded parents, it is better to get a couple of graduate degrees and take up teaching or else get a job in a political bureaucracy.

- Smile a lot.
- Never forget that promotions come from the kind of press you get from the people alongside of and below you. Toadying to bosses is self-destructive.
- Learn to type without looking at the keys.
- Choose hobbies or outside activities that involve meeting new people and keep it up all your business life.
- Always spell people's names right.
- Write. Write every day. Write to someone, about someone, even at someone.
- Read. Read a lot. Read everything. Don't skip the society section, the sports section, business section, or book reviews. Editorials, maybe.
- Learn to see the things you look at.
- Neatness counts.
- Don't get a reputation for last-minute work. Living dangerously destroys the confidence of clients, management, and anyone who takes Gelusil.
- Remember what your mother taught you to say—please, thank you, you're welcome. Also, gesundheit.
- Make your boss close the door, sit down with you, and talk over your progress, or lack thereof, once a year even if it embarrasses him. Or, increasingly, her.
- Worry a little, but not too much.
- Don't smoke pot in the office.

Nine Truths That Make Some People Uncomfortable

1. It is easier to get new business than to hold onto old business.

2. It is far more profitable to grow old accounts than to seek new ones.
3. No one will be interested in your business unless you are first interested in his.
4. If you don't understand the grammatical use of I, me, we, and us, talk about someone else.
5. It is not particularly difficult to write a good 60-second TV commercial. It is four times as hard to write a good 30-second commercial. It is 10 times as hard to write a good 10-second commerical. It is at least 500 times as hard to write a *great* commercial of any length.
6. It is much more difficult to write excellent industrial advertisements than consumer. It is much easier to write lousy industrial advertisements than consumer.
7. Nearly four-fifths of the *best* students getting advanced degrees in the best journalism and advertising colleges in the United States today are women.
8. Eighty percent of all surprises are unpleasant. This includes bills, estimates, unkept promises, firings, birthday parties and pregnancies.
9. No matter how many things have gone wrong in your life, be of good cheer because you ain't seen nothing yet.

How to Spot Losers. Winners, Too.

It's funny how often the service departments can figure out so quickly whether a new employee is going to make it or not. Usually long before the management makes its evaluation.

A few weeks ago, a young assistant account executive in one of our offices was dismissed because of accumulated lack of fantastic brilliance. No surprise to the media department. Soon after he arrived, he presented the media department with a list of more than 200 magazines, newspapers and trade journals with the request that they be instructed to put him on the complimentary list. The media department of course refused, and he got very iced up. Bye-bye.

In another office, I was waiting for the elevator near the switchboard. One operator said to another, "That _____, she's never at her desk. She *never* picks up a call!" I said to the office manager, "I hear _____ is not working out." He said it was news to him. About four weeks later her bosses decided she might as well spend her days at home as in our ladies' room.

In Chicago, my office is adjacent to the production department. In addition to overhearing a lot of Polish jokes, I also hear a lot of people trying to get an ad through. Some give orders, some make requests. Those that give orders often *become* a Polish joke.

It works both ways. The best Distant Early Warning system for spotting winners as well as losers is to listen to our support people—art, production, media, switchboard, receptionists, etc. When you hear admiration and praise from three or four such sources, get your bets down. Prejudice or romance may color the results of too small a sample, but when the unsolicited playback is all the same, you can make book.

Ultimately, even those of us laughingly described as management get the message.

Some Selected New Year's Resolutions for Some Unnamed Boors

After many years of making New Year's resolutions for myself, I've decided this year not to bother. At this advanced stage in life, I've decided there are a lot of people who need them more than I do.

So I've put down a few from which you are free to select, saving you the time required for self-analysis and original thinking, both painful pastimes at this period of the year. Help yourself.

- I resolve not to walk into someone's office when they're on the phone and stand there like a klutz, but to beat a well-mannered retreat and come back when the coast is clear and the collection agency has rung off.
- I resolve not to poke my head into offices with closed doors without knocking and waiting to be invited in, so that both naps and zipper repairs can be completed in peace.
- I resolve to take notes in meetings, even though I have 20-20 memory, just so the booby who is running the meeting will think I'm interested.
- I resolve not to interrupt someone else who is talking, unless it is a politician, a tax shelter shill, Gloria Steinem or a member of my immediate family.
- I resolve not to hold hands with manicurists or art directors, except for professional purposes.
- I resolve not to make snap judgments on men with either crew cuts or long hair, reserving my male hirsute bigotry exclusively to ponytails.
- I resolve to eat and drink less, even when someone else is buying.
- I resolve not to say "I can't" or "I haven't time" until I establish which it is—incompetence or lack of organization.

A Sense of the Imperative

Certain things drive clients nuts. Not the same things with all clients, but there are a few traits that will upset even the most understanding client.

Of these, the most frequent and correctable source of client-agency friction is delay—either from slow reaction or unkept promises. This is a common malady, and like pernicious anemia, once it settles into the system it is hard to reverse.

Creative Management

Every really successful advertising or public relations professional has a strong sense of urgency. The same is true of outstanding attorneys, doctors, public accountants, decorators, plumbers and prostitutes. Getting on with the job at hand is the "x" factor in the formula for success in the personal service business.

When I see a conference report issued a week after the meeting took place, I'm pretty sure that the assignments it records are already behind schedule. When I look at overtime reports, again and again I see profits drained away by frantic last minute rush, trying to make up for starting too late.

Sometimes, it's true, the fault is with the client, but far less frequently than we are inclined to claim. Again and again I've seen this situation: The same client, but a new account team; a chronic missed deadline problem ends overnight—or, quite the opposite, a steady on-time performance deteriorates suddenly. It's pretty hard in such cases to blame the client.

Actually, I have a lot of sympathy for clients, having been one for so long. Also, of course, I am still often in the role of client and I am not infrequently appalled at how long it takes to get a simple job done. Like any other client, when an assignment takes so long to complete, I tend to expect a particularly superb result, but disappointment is the usual outcome because the understanding we reached so long ago has become fogged by the lapse of time. A delayed job is rarely a good job. Often it is not even a usable job because along the way the objectives have been lost or changed, the strategy twisted and the mutual client-agency enthusiasm for the project has died of old age.

When we were starting this company, one account was Rockwell's Power Tool Division, then in Milwaukee, Wisconsin. The sales manager, like many Milwaukeeans, was of German descent. Every time we left him with a list of new assignments, his parting words were "Mach schnell!" Literal translation: "Make Fast!"

That's a great slogan for good client relations. A sense of the imperative is at least as important as a sense of smell when it comes to diffusing client unease.

126

Surprise! Surprise!

I hate surprises.

Years ago, the Chicago office decided to throw a surprise birthday party for me. While I was at lunch with a financial prospect we were wooing, my office was filled with balloons, hung with crepe paper and reorganized with a big chocolate cake as the centerpiece.

The lunch went well, and I got my starchy guest to walk back to look over some of our work and to tour the premises.

I simply adored it when I walked into my office and had a bag of confetti drop on my head from the doorjamb while my loved ones blew serpentine noisemakers in my face. Bailing out as best I could, I offered our prospect a piece of the cake, which turned out to be iced plywood. Funny, funny.

I don't like surprises.

Therefore, I'm very turned off if a client calls and says things aren't going well if it's the first I've heard of it. I don't like suppliers calling to say they can't get satisfaction on a disputed billing if I have none of the facts. I don't like to read about unbillable cost overruns that have been loosely covered by silence for six months because somebody was afraid to face facts.

In business and in life, things sometimes go wrong. I don't believe in public whippings ever or even private ones unless the problem happens often in the same place. In fact, we run the company on the assumption that good people, working at a busy pace, are going to drop a stitch now and then.

All we really ask is that when a stitch *is* missed, it is pointed out so that we can unravel a few rows instead of the whole sweater.

Trouble inevitably comes from burying mistakes in shallow graves. The least little trampling around uncovers them, and attention is diverted from the simple mistake to the act of subterfuge, and that destroys confidence.

If something goes wrong, if you're overloaded and getting dangerously behind, if there are storm signals in client or supplier relations, the way to be a hero (heroine?) is to go to your boss and get it out in the open quickly.

None of us can be perfect. All of us can be straight-forward.

How to Work a Party

Unlike many of my crochety generation, I believe that, taken as a group, our young today are brighter, more ethical, and better educated than we were.

Of course, there are some really egocentric smarties among them, but probably there's little choice between a self-assured ding-a-ling and a humble ding-a-ling.

I do fear, however, that we're running short of people with the social graces that smooth the human relations of commerce.

I am frequently appalled at receptions, cocktail parties, lunches, dinners and other business/social functions at how few people seem to have given any thought to the purpose of such a planned scrambling and know how to act.

It starts with understanding that, in most cases, the affair wasn't given for your benefit but rather, usually, you are an assistant host or hostess. Most of these convocations wouldn't be happening if there wasn't a business relationship and therefore your presence is an extension of your job.

That is true whether it's a client or supplier affair, or even a strictly in-house activity. And it's true even if there are higher-ranking managers on the premises, not all of whom are so socially deft either. Here are some simple rules that can't hurt and usually will put everyone at ease, including you.

- Mingle. Above all don't spend your time with the people from your office.
- Introduce people. Use full names. Never, "Bill, this is Lois." Above all, never, "You know each

other, don't you?" Never take it for granted that people remember each other's names—people are not embarrassed by having their names repeated, but they can be made to look bad by leaving them groping.

- Rescue anyone standing around alone.
- Move in on groups composed entirely of guests.
- Don't stand around with your thumb up your nose waiting for someone to get you a drink. Rather, see if you can get a drink for a guest, or help pass the chutney-stuffed popcorn balls.
- Unless there is preplanned seating, figure out with whom you'll sit so we don't wind up with them-and-us table arrangements.
- If it's a husband and wife thing, encourage your spouse to shuffle around, too.
- Best of all, for any major function, have a preview meeting of our team to review who's coming, what their interests are, who'll be responsible for whom, correct pronunciation of names, etc. You'll be much more relaxed if you do.

Now with all this coaching, you are well prepared to spill drinks, drop the dip, introduce two of our own people to each other in front of a client and mistake a guest for a waiter as proficiently as anyone.

Left-Over Thoughts on Professional Communications

"It was words—great inflammatory, action words—that converted a mob that cheered Caesar's murder into one that pursued Brutus to his death."

(Author Unknown)

Creative Management

As you know, Elias Howe invented the sewing machine. What the history books overlook is that he couldn't get anyone to buy it. He was so unsuccessful commercially that he had to borrow a suit to go to his wife's funeral. He was ahead of his time, not with his invention, but because he had no understanding of how to explain the sewing machine to prospective buyers—there was no concept of advertising to tell its benefits in terms of labor saving and a better life, and it limped along with very little attention for years. A whole generation of women lived and died without ever knowing it existed, and their lives and their families' lives were the more drab because there was no public notice of it.

* * * *

When I was a young man, the popular definition of advertising was that it was salesmanship in print. That is a definition with blinders, even if you add the electronic media that have come along since then. Advertising is simply a form of communication. It can work in concert with or instead of or even in opposition to publicity and public relations, word of mouth, unsponsored observation and even such subtle communicators as smell and feel.

It is no longer enough to know how advertising works; it is imperative to understand and be able to choose among the alternative routes of communication.

* * * *

The worst waste in advertising is dropping a successful campaign just when it is beginning to build an audience or increase inquiries or influence direct sales.

Stopping advertising campaigns yearly and starting over is like reading half of a mystery story and then starting a new one—you never know for sure how it will come out. The purpose is never quite fulfilled.

* * * *

The best advertising is fairly simple and proceeds step by step from an interesting start to a logical conclusion. Sometimes it is a long walk and sometimes a short walk, but with good advertising the direction, the pace and the purpose are easy to trace.

* * * *

Here is a wonderful commentary on the information function of advertising. One of the most insidious critics of advertising is a man named Vance Packard. He wrote a book called "Hidden Persuaders," which leveled a loaded attack on advertising. It became something of a bestseller. But how did people get to know about it?

It was widely advertised in newspapers and magazines across the country. Advertising was the only way the publishers knew to sell a book attacking the means by which it was sold!

* * * *

Industrial marketing today is much more complex, made so by complex technologies and by complicated ways of looking at problems. The man who once said, "I need a ¾"-inch bolt," now says, "I need a way of fastening these parts."

* * * *

We have always had the choice, given a promotion budget of X amount, of spending it on trade papers, consumer publications, trade shows, catalogs, publicity, radio, and so on, in any combination of any amounts. Our decisions were compounded of the past, prejudice, pressure and politics.

For most of us this is still true, but not for long. Lots of quiet experimentation is going on in marketing simulation and the development of marketing matrices to test out various combinations. It may turn out after all these years that another page of space is better than another case of whisky for the Kansas City salesman. Of course, it may not, too.

But the upshot will be that the ultimate allocation of resources will have all communications working together, not conceived and executed by separate people for separate objectives, sometimes jealously defended against reason.

What We Believe

According to legend, J. Walter Thompson, the founder of the advertising agency that took his name, was a rather formal, aloof and dignified man.

One hot summer afternoon, years ago, he was riding uptown on the old New York Third Avenue El when a frowzy bum smelling of the Bowery and the brewery sat down beside him. The man was struggling with a set of sandwich boards, the kind of front-and-back signs derelicts were paid 25 cents a day to wear walking around the streets.

Mr. Thompson, very uncomfortable but more or less trapped, tried to ignore the man, but the bum kept trying to start a conversation. Finally he asked, "What business are you in?"

Mr. Thompson, who was known as a dedicated evangelist for his business, said, "Advertising!"

The bum reached across to shake his hand.

"Me, too," he said, "and ain't it hell when the wind blows?"

As long as I have been in advertising, there have been winds. They come from government, education, or pockets of extemporaneous criticism. Sometimes they kick up swirls of sand that sting but die down when the facts become visible. Sometimes, however, they cut to the bone.

We should be concerned that these winds seem to have a demoralizing effect on some people in our business, especially some of our young people. I think they need the assurance that comes from a reexamination of the fundamentals that underlie the successful creation of advertising.

This is what we have been saying to our young people:

We are in the business of communicating. We believe that it is a good and honorable and useful occupation. As much so as law, accounting or investment banking.

It can be practiced with high standards or low standards or no standards.

We believe it can be pursued conscientiously or care-

134

lessly, as surely as farming, or forestry, or medicine, or editing, or teaching.

We believe that neither excellence nor mediocrity are endemic to our business, and while it undoubtedly is a business and not a profession, it can be practiced professionally.

To do this—to act like professionals and to maintain professional standards—we believe that companies and their people must come to grips with what they want to be, how they want to be known, what goals they seek and how they expect to achieve them.

Consequently, as one microcosm in the world of advertising and public relations, we have our own commitments. While they are ours, we suggest that if they are instilled in the young people coming into the business, they will remove many of the tensions between this business and the consumer, or between this business and government, or between our business and academia.

Our beliefs fall into several categories.

The first are ethical beliefs. We tell our people that everything they do must be honest. We tell them to ask themselves: If this were my company, would I spend my own money this way?

We believe that it is not enough merely to maintain our own standards. We believe we must do what we can to raise our voices on behalf of high ethical standards for our entire industry. What hurts the industry hurts us.

The second set of beliefs to which we cling has to do with our product. One of the charms of advertising is that it is a business of infinite choice. There are always many ways to communicate, many ways to express an idea, so it is easy to be dissatisfied. It's quite realistic to say that what we did today is not good enough and that we can do it better. Therefore, dissatisfaction with the merely adequate can become a practical way of life.

The advertising business rewards certain types of people with certain outlooks. Among the generous fringe benefits are money, pride, happiness, and association with remarkably interesting people.

Creative Management

It's my observation that in this world only a few people are equipped to handle ideas with skill and pleasure. This business sours some. It attracts some cynics who, when they smell flowers, immediately look for the coffin. Nevertheless, it is a business peculiarly conducive to maintaining a climate of achievement if you want to do so.

For every right that you cherish, we tell our people, you have a duty you must fulfill. For every hope that you entertain, you have a task you must perform. For every good you wish to preserve, you'll have to sacrifice comfort. There is nothing for nothing.

Cezanne painted some fruit, a bowl and a jug again and again and again, in different arrangements as thousands of painters before and after him have done, but he is the master. Why? Mostly because after each of the thousands of strokes he would clean his brush to get exact shadings, pure colors and a perfectly even layer of paint.

It is axiomatic that advertising will always be subject to a series of shifting criticisms. I believe we are best able to deal with outside criticism if we continuously practice self-criticism. If we do, we will be better able to give it as well as take it.

This business needs a special kind of people. It needs people who have their heads in the clouds and their feet in the cash box.

And, if we are to be above and ahead of our critics, we must constantly work at maintaining an industry-wide environment of excellence.

Excellence is not reserved for the favored few. It is available to all who are willing to unlock the power, beauty, daring and infinite imagination that reside in the human mind and human spirit.

Excellence is many things.

It is people who care, people who aspire, people who suffer, people who succeed, people who are dissatisfied, and

Therefore, people who aspire, people who suffer, people who succeed, people who are dissatisfied, and on, and on, and on.

136

I'm Afraid I Don't Understand You (And Maybe I Don't Even Want To)*

There is a widely held theory that new technologies in instantaneous international communications will bring universal understanding and peace in our time.

I wish I believed this. If it is true, then those of us who make our living as self-licensed experts in the arts of communications will be the saviors of the world. The facts, I fear, are that the satellite systems and other marvelous transmittal developments may prove only how little anyone really knows about the communication of understanding.

For example, there's a good likelihood that a fair number of our clients and prospects think differently than we do about what the word "communications" means.

In trying to define what our advertising agency believes is its Unique Selling Proposition, we say we are in the business of Total Communications. That would amuse Western Union, or NBC, or the *Chicago Tribune*, since we send no wires, broadcast no television programs and print no newspapers. But compared to a lot of other advertising agencies, we perform a much wider range of communications chores, so we go about the land selling our skills at Total Communications, perhaps confusing everyone but ourselves.

That's a nice little lesson in one of the biggest barriers you and I have to effective communications—assuming other people understand what we are talking about simply because it is so clear to us.

So many things get in the way of communication and so many of them are so deeply rooted and so indelibly a part of our individual character that it is almost impossible to divorce one's self from the impediments to understanding. Some are simple to recognize, but some are as subtle as the virus structure of the common cold and equally widespread.

---

*From "The Wonderful World of Words."

So let's start with language, one of the simpler blocks to communication. If I speak English and you speak French, you do not understand me unless you are bilingual. But even if you are an English-speaking Frenchman, you may understand my words yet miss my point entirely. Take the famous Volkswagen ad which was headed "Lemon." One of my French friends who speaks quite good English could make no sense of it. The idea simply doesn't translate into French because there is no environmental framework for the idea that an inferior product is a "lemon" or indeed for the concept that any manufacturer would admit that he occasionally produced a bad product, even if he caught it before it was sold.

A few years ago, we were working with IBM World Trade developing a new campaign that was to run world-wide in 16 languages. We were trying to find a way to say that IBM's problem-solving capabilities were available equally in all those countries in which advertising was to run and that the kinds of problems to which the computers were adaptable were omnipresent.

We came up with a common theme—"Problems Know No Nationality." To our surprise, we found that the word "nationality" doesn't translate uniformly at all and that what were were saying was subject to many interpretations, not all favorable. We finally settled on "Problems Know No Boundaries," which is less precise in English but more nearly what we were trying to say in other languages.

More than one fine sales proposition has run into trouble when the language changes. I am told that the once-powerful Avis "No. 2" program, while it translates, doesn't work in some countries where there is no traditional sympathy for the underdog, a trait of character so universally held in the United States that the point Avis was trying to make comes across to nearly all of us with the same shade of meaning.

Even within the same language are all kinds of hidden turns.

Some years ago the head of a large English advertising agency came to visit me. He brought out a notebook in which, to save our time, he had written a series of questions about our company, but first he said, "Some of these questions are a bit cheeky and I have no doubt that in some cases you will want to say that it is none of my business. Please do, in any such instance, and I will quite understand."

I told him I was prepared to be perfectly frank and that he need feel no reticence.

His first question was, "What is your turnover?"

Well, I explained to him that I understood why he would ask that first, what with all the publicity given to the high turnover of American advertising agencies. However, I explained, we were proud of the fact that ours was so small at that time that it simply made no sense to bother to keep formal records on it and so I was simply unable to answer.

He said, "Well, if you have such a small turnover, how do you operate a business of this apparent size?"

You have to be modest in a situation like that, so I said, "Oh, no one thing. A lot of things, really."

And he said, "You know, old chap, I don't mean to pry and, as I said first off, I understand that you may wish to tell me to mind my own bloody business!"

I told him that wasn't it at all; I simply didn't know. To ease the tension, I said to him: "Mr. Fielding, what is *your* turnover?"

"Twelve million pounds," he answered.

And suddenly I remembered having read that in England sales are stated as turnover.

There are so many traps. I know an American company that set up a Canadian subsidiary a few years ago. They'd read a good deal about anti-American feeling in Canada, so they obscured the American parentage in the subsidiary name, rechristened the products and began advertising. Their advertising people, to save time and expense, simply picked up the copy intact from U.S. advertising and were surprised when they got two letters asking what U.S. company they were representing, since it was clear the promotion was originating below the border inasmuch as "flavor" and "savor" were both spelled without the "u."

Even in more homogeneous groups there are so many

impediments to understanding. You have seen the word list test where you are asked to write down the first word you think of that most nearly associates in your mind with the test word (Table: chair; Red: green). Have you ever taken one with your wife or husband and compared your answers? How can two people live together for 25 years, apparently in communication with one another, and have less than a 50 percent correlation?

In pretesting advertising, we run into these differences constantly. Bring 50 housewives together, show them a series of TV commercials, and ask them to play back to you what they understood the commercials to say. If you wrote the commercial, content in the belief that you have been simple, convincing, perhaps amusing, you are likely to be very distressed at the results. It sometimes seems impossible that the message could have strayed so far.

And if you think it is explained by the fact that these are emotional women, our research shows that the risks are just as great with machine tool advertising aimed at presumably logical engineers.

Yet, easy as it is to overlook these communications barriers, they are the relatively more simple ones to deal with.

The common pretest is the best way and it can take many forms. A pilot study before the market research questionnaire is sent out broadcast. Rehearsal of your sales presentation before a small group of our own people to get their reactions. Feedback studies of advertising and public relations to find out what understanding the audience plays back.

Once upon a time, if I wrote or said something that was misunderstood, I used to argue about what I was trying to say. Now I just give up and try to say it differently. I'd rather argue about what I believe than what I mean.

Actually, the biggest obstruction to true communication is what we believe. The interpreters at the United Nations can change the language, but they can't change beliefs. Hospitality, cordiality and wine can change the atmosphere without rooting out old beliefs. The incredible generosity of our foreign aid program may have prevented revolutions, and, as a compassionate measure in a starving world it may be justified, but there is little evidence that it has had much success in changing beliefs.

Even with people you know well, there may be a barricade to belief.

At the start of World War II, I was involved in personnel work at a nonunion manufacturing plant in the Northern Indiana steelmaking area. It was a relatively small company and I knew everyone who worked there. I played golf in the plant golf league. I drank beer with the machinists and welders and forge shop men in the local saloons because I liked them. I went to their Polish, Italian and Greek weddings and was called upon to say a few words as "a friend of the groom."

Then one day the massive wave of the United Steelworkers, CIO, reached our plant door and, after a couple of inconclusive elections, we had a union. Suddenly I was sitting on the other side of a bargaining table and suddenly I realized that underneath it all they didn't quite trust me. At some point their basic beliefs about capital and labor filtered conviction out of our communication.

So many little things get us in trouble. Perhaps you remember the sad story of misunderstanding between Eastman Kodak Company and the Rochester, New York, black community. It is reported that, at a key point in the discussions, when it looked like things were pretty well worked out and the black leaders seemed to be convinced of Eastman's good faith, an Eastman official started out, "You boys. . . . "

Such an easy mistake! The president of the National Association of Manufacturers could say it to his board of directors and they would never notice it, much less revolt. But to a people with a deep resentment of having the bossman address them as "boy" even if they were 70, it was an affront of tragic dimensions and meaningful communications ended.

Another thing that gets in the way of communication is authorship. I've seen a test in which a statement on economics was given to a group of union members and they were asked if they agreed with it. The statement was signed George Meany, President of the AFL-CIO. More than 75 percent of the union members said they agreed. The same statement was given to a similar number of members from the same union, only this time it was attributed to Roger Blough, chairman of U.S. Steel. This time over 70 percent disagreed.

Then there are selfish barriers to communication, best described by these statements:

"This is the way *I* see it."

"I know what interests *me*."

An awful lot of corporate or institutional advertising ends up near total waste because of this approach. The way you see it is rarely the way the other fellow sees it, especially if you are the seller and he is the buyer, because you're standing at a different angle from the start. What interests you most often interests your prospects least. Every advertising and public relations man has had the problem of trying to dissuade a client from running a picture of his new plant with all his 25-year employees in front, and his products across the bottom. The word "Quality" will be prominent in the headline.

It's interesting about "quality." It is one of a group of words that is almost useless in real communication. They are worn out and they meld into the crowd of words so you don't notice them. "Rugged" construction. What does it mean? "Extra" strength. You pass them by in everyone else's ads, yet so many writers of advertising and PR sprinkle them through their own copy.

All of this may sound negative and pessimistic, but of course we're constantly learning more about communicating understanding.

We're learning the power of words. We know more about using the basic drives and self-interests of the audience. We are becoming better at picking a posture—of modesty, on the one hand, or authority, on the other—for consistency of impact. We're learning the value of testing, the trial balloon, and rehearsal.

While words—and of course pictures, which have character and mood, too—are extremely useful, they are tools but not the craft itself.

The craft is harder to describe. Much of it is intuitive, as for instance when to be modest and when to be authoritative. The Avis campaign was a classic case of using a modest approach to disarm the audience and make it receptive for the real message. The message was not that Avis is No. 2. The message Avis was communicating was that you'll get a cleaner, better-serviced car with less waiting. Advertisers are not often modest—in fact most people are not really very modest when talking about themselves—and there is somehow an air of believability and trust in modesty if it seems genuine.

On the other hand, matter-of-fact authority has its place, too. I have a friend, a research man who is well known and respected for the work he has done on magazine readership. Once, in a speech before a group of normally cynical agency media people, he said, among other things, that readership of trade and technical papers did not drop off in the summertime. One of the audience challenged him. "On what authority do you make that statement?" Although my friend had at that time done no real research on the subject and had no proof, he said, "On my own authority." To his surprise, his questioner sat down and everyone accepted the statement as fact. In the same vein, when General Eisenhower was President, students of his press conferences noted that he was rarely heckled on military matters, on which he was sometimes out of date, but was often questioned quite skeptically concerning domestic matters, on which he was often very well prepared.

One of the techniques that becomes a part of the craft of communication is simply reporting. Called by fancier, more salable names, it is sometimes described as an attitude audit or audience appraisal. It is nothing more than asking penetrating questions of the customers and prospects for a product, a company or an industry and finding out what they now know, what they want to know—what turns them on or off. This is then laid alongside what the company or industry wants to say about itself. Whether there is meaningful communication depends upon whether the two can be made compatible.

Then there are the basic human drives that aid or impede communication. Perfume is a form of communication. Bacon cooking communicates. The Playboy bunnies, wiggling their cotton tails, communicate. The trick is to be aware of all the senses and all the routes of communication to the images of the senses.

There is no better way to find out if you have communicated than to ask someone to play back to you what you have said or written. Good advertising is usually checked in this way. George Gallup has parlayed poll taking into a big business of reporting advertising impact.

Good sales presentations should be tested, too.

All presentations should be rehearsed before a live and critical audience. If you are going to make a sales call, make it first in your office and develop an atmosphere that encourages your associates to be critical of each other. Don't worry about form or manners; worry about whether your point is getting across. Do other people understand you? When the man says, "I'm afraid I don't understand you," he is also saying under his breath, "And maybe I don't even want to."

When you come right down to it, the art of communications is the ability, which positively can be cultivated, of automatically thinking in terms of the audience instead of yourself. It is the ultimately instinctive habit of telling me what you are going to do for me before you ask me to do anything at all for you. It is the ability to be genuinely interested in other people and other people's interests.

It is, in short, the art of selflessness.

Games People Play

One of the tough things about this business is becoming someone else, thinking, feeling, reacting like someone who has a totally different heredity and environment.

Yet success in almost any function in our business is in part directly related to the ability to fantasize yourself into becoming someone else.

If you are trying to place a story in, say, *Institutions*, you have to first become, in your imagination, an *Institutions* reader—a restaurant manager, a hospital dietician—whatever.

If you are trying to sell yogurt in Chicago, you have to mentally move to Chicago, where supermarkets have different names than in New York, where the ethnic mix and traditions are different, where deeply ingrained eating habits are not quite like those in the East or West or South.

If you expect to sell (change minds, reinforce convictions), you must, as Willy Loman said, know the territory.

The territory for tourists is lakes and buildings and museums and hotels, but the territory for the communications business is people.

Long ago I learned the most fascinating game of solitaire you can play is to close your eyes and be someone else somewhere else.

What would your day be like, you can ask yourself to suppose, if you were a farmer in Kansas? A banker in Brussels? A professor at the University of California?

What would you be doing now if you were a doctor with a busy urban practice?

Where would your wife shop if you lived in rural England? Or rural West Virginia?

What kind of person would you be if you were chief engineer of a power generating station? Or a postman? Policeman? Or a fashion model, age 19? Or a fashion model, age 32? What hangups, what prejudices, what kind of friends would you have?

When my kids were little, on a long car trip after a half hour of "My Father Has a Grocery Store and In It He Sells S . . . ," we would sometimes play "Living Someone Else's Life." It is an adult game for children, or perhaps the other way around, but it is endlessly wonderful to anyone who can dream, to anyone who likes people, to anyone filled with the wonder of being unique and alive. The permutations are endless.

It is a learning game, too, in that it exercises and develops the senses and therefore develops sensitivity. The textbook is simply acute observation—a restless interest in other people, other places, other triumphs, other defeats, other goals and beliefs and satisfactions. Its aim is not judgment but understanding.

And the prize is a broader vision of what business is really all about.

Smart Clients

While I've now been an agent for 29 years, before that I was a client for ten. I'm sure I was just as smart a client as an agent.

I've never been sure why it is that working for an agency turns some people into supercilious self-designated experts who go around belching sour disdain for the clients who pay the bills. Of course they are a minority or the clients would pull our business down around us. Yet no corporate contraceptives seem to be completely effective in keeping these client baiters from reproducing.

When I was a client, my agencies brought me some bad ideas mixed in with the good; once in a while they proposed a promotion that simply didn't conform to our corporate style; now and then I turned down work because the writing seemed leaden or the pictures, in my view, were below what I perceived as a proper level of interest or excitement. These were very subjective judgments I was making and often I had trouble putting my rejection into a clear, logical explanation. Yet I never felt I was exceeding my prerogatives, nor did I lose sleep over being somewhat arbitrary. Much art, music, and writing is born in a "feel" or concept or vision that is hard for the creator to explain. The customer or client or patron will also have difficulty at times communicating the reasons for either enthusiastic acceptance or hesitant rejection.

146

Let's say, for example, that we're dealing with the introduction to the public of a new line of horizontally striped pantyhose. A team of our brightest and best put together a detailed program, but after careful consideration the client is uneasy with some of our recommendations and asks us to try again. He can't completely document his resistance, but in trying to do so he makes several suggestions of his own that don't do much to stoke our fires.

Assuming that he's normally intelligent, motivated by a desire for his company's success, we should respect his complete right to say "no." There must be hundreds—more likely, thousands—of exciting ideas to bring the product to the market and we would be fools to say that any two or three are far better than all the others.

As experience grows, I have come to listen more and more closely to clients. All but a few, I find, are smart. Their point of view is often different from ours and that's good, not bad. I think that most often the quickest way to zero in on the bull's-eye is to find out where the client's point of view and ours intersect.

The Great Accomplishments of a Full Life

Looking backward, as great philosophers from Socrates to Satchel Paige have said, is a deady diversion, a signal of decline. Life is always in a forward direction.

Yet most of us sneak a peek over our shoulder now and then, especially to relive our finest hours. After all, the richest reward of striving is accomplishment.

I have had some extraordinarily satisfying triumphs. I hope you'll forgive my immodesty in sharing them with you. Among the ones I remember most happily and vividly are these:

- While still in grammar school, filling in for John Philip Sousa to finish a concert of his famous marching band by conducting a finale of "Stars and Stripes Forever."

- The tumultuous applause after my performance of the Brahms B Flat concerto at Orchestra Hall with the Chicago Symphony, Fritz Reiner conducting.
- Mingling with the audience after the opening of "Kismet," hearing people humming Borodin's music and singing my lyrics.
- Skating in practice with the Chicago Black Hawk hockey team.
- Telling Maurice Stans, who was calling from Washington, that I would not contribute to the Committee to Reelect.
- Accepting the invitation of the chef of the Tour d'Argent in Paris to critique his preparation of Sole Cardinale.
- Blushing at the standing ovation after a speech before the American Association of Advertising Agencies.
- Getting a hole-in-one with my entire family, Vice President Nixon, and Bebe Rebozo watching.
- A 14-point bold by-line centered over a three-column lead story on the front page of the Chicago *Daily News*.
- Waltzing in Vienna while other dancers, couple by couple, stopped to watch.
- Being awakened from a sound sleep at the Beverly Wilshire Hotel by persistent knocking, to open the door and find Elizabeth Taylor there, wanting to come in, and telling her to go away, that I was too tired.

You may find it hard to believe that all these things really happened. I'm certain that some of them did but they are all so clear in my mind and my emotions that it's hard to be sure of the exact facts.

The point is, they all add a dimension to my life. Sometimes there is a foggy barrier between what you want to do and what you are able to do. Some great force, in designing man, built in the power of imagination. It is there in all of us, strongly developed by constant exercise, or made flabby by repression and disuse.

Imagination is an expression of freedom and joy. It is the heartbeat of creativity.

It is, therefore, a concomitant to success in our business. And many other businesses.

The Wonderful World of Words*

Human beings come in all sizes, a variety of colors, in different ages, and with unique, complex, and changing personalities.

So do words.

There are tall, skinny words and short, fat ones, and strong ones and weak ones, and boy words and girl words, and so on.

For instance, title, lattice, latitude, lily, tattle, Illinois and intellect are all lean and lanky. While these words get their height partly from "t's" and "l's," other words are tall and skinny without a lot of ascenders and descenders. Take, for example, Abraham, peninsula and elipsis, all tall.

Here are some nice short, fat words: hog, yogurt, bomb, pot, bonbon, acne, plump, sop and slobber.

Sometimes a word gets its size from what it means, but sometimes it's just how the word sounds. Acne is a short, fat word even though pimple, with which it is associated, is a puny word.

There's a difference between tall, skinny words and puny words. Totter is out-and-out puny, while teeter is more just slender. Tea, tepid, stool and weary are puny.

---

*From "The Wonderful World of Words."

Puny words are not the same as feminine words. Feminine words are such as tissue, slipper, cute, squeamish, peek, flutter, gauze and cumulus. Masculine words are like bourbon, rupture, oak, cartel, steak and socks. Words can mean the same thing and be of the opposite sex. Naked is masculine, but nude is feminine.

Sex isn't always a clear-cut, yes-or-no thing, and there are words like that too. On a fencing team, for instance, a man may compete with a sabre and that is definitely a masculine word. Because it is also a sword of sorts, an epee is also a boy word, but you know how it is with epees.

Just as feminine words are not necessarily puny words, masculine words are not necessarily muscular. Muscular words are thrust, earth, girder, ingot, cask, Leo, ale, bulldozer, sledge and thug. Fullback is very muscular; quarterback is masculine but not especially muscular.

Words have colors, too. To wit:

- Red: fire, passion, explode, smash, murder, rape, lightning, attack.
- Green: moss, brook, cool, comfort, meander, solitude, hammock.
- Black: glower, agitate, funeral, dictator, anarchy, thunder, tomb, somber, cloak.
- Beige: unctuous, abstruse, surrender, clerk, conform, observe, float.

San Francisco is a red city, Cleveland is beige, Asheville is green and Buffalo is black.

Shout is red, persuade is green, rave is black and listen is beige.

Oklahoma is brown, Florida is yellow, Virginia is light blue and Massachusetts is dark green, almost black. Although they were all Reds, Khruschev was red-red, Castro orange, Mao Tse-tung gray, and Kadar black as hate.

One of the more useful characteristics of words is their age.

There's youth in go, pancake, hamburger, bat, ball, frog, air, surprise, morning and tickle. Middle age brings abrupt, moderate, agree, shade, stroll and uncertain. Fragile, lavender, astringent, acerbic, fern, velvet, lace, worn and Packard are old. There never was a young Packard, not even the touring car.

Mostly, religion is old. Prayer, vespers, choir, Joshua, Judges, Ruth and cathedral are all old. Once temple was older than cathedral, and it still is in some parts of the world, but in the United States, temple is now fairly young. Rocker is younger than it used to be, since President Kennedy.

Saturday, the seventh day of the week, is young while Sunday, the first day of the week, is old. Night is old, and so although more old people die in the hours of the morning just before the dawn, we call that part of the morning, incorrectly, night.

Some words are worried and some radiate disgusting self-confidence. Pill, ulcer, twitch, itch, stomach and peek are all worried words. Confident, smug words are like proud, lavish, major, divine, stare, dare, ignore, demand. Suburb used to be a smug word and still is in some parts of the country, but not so much around New York anymore. Brooklyn, by the way, is a confident word and everyone knows the Bronx is a worried word. Joe is confident; Horace is worried.

Now about shapes.

For round products, round companies or round ideas use dot, bob, melon, loquacious, hock, bubble and bald. Square words are, for instance, box, cramp, sunk, block and even ankle. Ohio is round but Iowa, a similar word, is square but not as square as Nebraska. The roundest city is, of course, Oslo.

Some words are clearly oblong. Obscure is oblong (it is also beige) and so are platter and meditation (which is also middle-aged). Lavish, which as we say is self-confident, is also oblong. The most oblong lake is Ontario, even more oblong than Michigan, which is surprisingly muscular for an oblong, though, of course, not nearly as strong as Huron, which is more stocky. Lake Pontchartrain is almost a straight line. Lake Como is round and very short and fat; Lake Erie is worried.

Some words are shaped like Rorschach ink blots. Like drool, plot, mediocre, involvement, liquid, amoeba and phlegm.

At first blush (which is young), fast words seem to come from a common stem (which is puny). For example, dash, flash, bash, and brash are all fast words. However, ash, hash and gnash are all slow. Flush is changing. It used to be slow, somewhat like sluice, but it is getting faster. Both are wet words, as is Flushing, which is really quite dry compared to New Canaan, which sounds drier but is much wetter. Wilkinsburg, as you would expect, is dry, square, old and light gray. But back to motion.

Raid, rocket, piccolo, hound, bee and rob are fast words. Guard, drizzle, lard, cow, sloth, muck and damp are slow words. Fast words are often young and slow words old, but not always. Hamburger is young but slow, especially when uncooked. Astringent is old but fast. Black is old, and yellow—nearly opposite on the spectrum—is young, but orange and brown are nearly next to each other and orange is just as young as yellow, while brown is only middle-aged. Further, purple, though darker than lavender, is not as old; however, it is much slower than violet, which is extremely fast.

Because it's darker, purple is often softer than lavender, even though it is younger. Lavender is actually a rather hard word. Not as hard as rock, edge, point, corner, jaw, trooper, frigid or trumpet, but hard nevertheless. Lamb, lip, thud, sofa, fuzz, stuff, froth and madam are soft. Although they are the same thing, timpani are harder than kettle drums, partly because drum is a soft word (it is also fat and slow) and as pots and pans go, kettle is one of the softer.

Sometimes word images are too complex to put into rigid categories. They simply come through as a whole idea.

For instance, many people have talked about Batten, Barton, Durstine and Osborn being like a trunk bouncing down a flight of stairs. Ogilvy & Mather is like tea time at tweedy tailor's. Ruder & Finn is like mice running in the kitchen when you turn on the lights. Ketchum, MacLeod &

Grove is vegetable-beef soup with barley. Hill & Knowlton is a beautifully printed house organ that nobody reads but many people save. G. M. Basford was an old Pullman car with stale cigarette smoke. N. W. Ayer is an Episcopalian prayer. J. Walter Thompson is a man getting his picture taken between Charles Evans Hughes and William Howard Taft. Interpublic, Inc., is a chain of turnpike pay toilets.

There is a point to all of this.

Ours is a business of imagination. We are employed to make faceless companies personable, to make useful products desirable, to clarify ideas, to create friendships in the mass for our employers.

We have great power to do these things. We have power through art and photography and graphics and typography and all the visual elements that are part of the finished advertisement or commercial, or the published publicity release.

And these are great powers. Often it is true that one picture is worth ten thousand words.

But not necessarily worth one word if it's the right one.